McDougal Littell
Pre-Algebra

Larson   Boswell   Kanold   Stiff

Justin Hissey 7B

Practice Workbook

The Practice Workbook provides additional practice for every lesson in the textbook. The workbook covers essential vocabulary, skills, and problem solving. Space is provided for students to show their work.

Justin Hissey

McDougal Littell
A DIVISION OF HOUGHTON MIFFLIN COMPANY
Evanston, Illinois • Boston • Dallas

Contents

Chapter

1	Practice for Lessons 1.1–1.8	1–16
2	Practice for Lessons 2.1–2.7	17–30
3	Practice for Lessons 3.1–3.6	31–42
4	Practice for Lessons 4.1–4.7	43–56
5	Practice for Lessons 5.1–5.7	57–70
6	Practice for Lessons 6.1–6.8	71–86
7	Practice for Lessons 7.1–7.7	87–100
8	Practice for Lessons 8.1–8.9	101–118
9	Practice for Lessons 9.1–9.8	119–134
10	Practice for Lessons 10.1–10.8	135–150
11	Practice for Lessons 11.1–11.9	151–168
12	Practice for Lessons 12.1–12.8	169–184
13	Practice for Lessons 13.1–13.7	185–198

Name _____ Date _____

Practice

For use with pages 5–9

Evaluate the expression when y = 6.

1. $\dfrac{24}{y}$

2. $5y$

3. $20 - y$

4. $19 + y$

5. $y + 13$

6. $54 - y$

7. $7y$

8. $\dfrac{36}{y}$

Evaluate the expression when m = 7, n = 9, and q = 10.

9. nq

10. $\dfrac{18}{n}$

11. $m + q$

12. $29 - m$

13. $58 - m$

14. $41 + n$

15. $16q$

16. $\dfrac{36}{n}$

17. You are dividing 130 students into g equally sized groups for a field trip. Write a variable expression to find the number of students in each group.

Name _____ Date _____

Practice

For use with pages 5–9

Write a variable expression to represent the phrase.

18. A number added to 27

19. 29 decreased by a number

20. 6 fewer than a number

21. The sum of 16 and a number

22. The product of a number and 7

23. 42 divided by a number

24. The quotient of 56 and a number

25. A number multiplied by 12

In Exercises 26–29, use the following information. You belong to a book club. Your yearly book budget is $350. Each book in the book club costs $7.

26. Complete the table.

Books	Cost (dollars)	Amount left (dollars)
1	7	343
2	14	336
3		
4		

27. Write a variable expression for the cost of *b* books.

28. Write a variable expression for the amount of your budget after *b* books.

29. How many books will you be able to buy before the $350 is spent?

Name _____ Date _____

Practice

For use with pages 10–13

Write the product using an exponent.

1. $43 \cdot 43 \cdot 43 \cdot 43$

2. $100 \cdot 100 \cdot 100$

3. $x \cdot x \cdot x$

4. $p \cdot p \cdot p \cdot p \cdot p$

Evaluate the expression when $n = 8$ and $n = 0.3$.

5. n^2

6. n^3

7. n^4

8. n^6

9. n^8

10. n^7

Write the power in words and as a repeated multiplication. Then evaluate the power.

11. 9^6

12. 16^4

13. 2.5^4

14. 1.4^3

Evaluate the expression when $x = 0.64$ and $y = 15$.

15. x^3

16. x^2

17. x^1

18. y^3

19. y^4

20. y^5

Pre-Algebra
Chapter 1   Practice Workbook

Name _____ Date _____

Practice

For use with pages 10–13

Find the area of the square.

21.
17 in.

22.
22 ft

23.
2.5 m

24.
0.6 cm

Find the volume of the cube.

25.
0.9 yd

26.
1.3 ft

27.
30 cm

28.
18 mm

29. Compare each number in the top row of the table with the number below it. Describe any pattern you see. Complete the table with a variable expression involving *n*.

1	2	3	4	$\cdots$	*n*
1	16	81	256	$\cdots$	

Name _____ Date _____

Practice
For use with pages 16–21

Evaluate the expression.

1. $6.1(4) + 2(1.5)$

2. $58.4 - 4(9.2)$

3. $\dfrac{2.6 + 3.9}{7.8 - 7.3}$

4. $\dfrac{42 - 17}{0.2(25)}$

5. $7(16 - 2^3)$

6. $9(3 + 5^3)$

7. $2.5[10 + (20 - 2^2)]$

8. $3.1[100 - (5^2 \cdot 3)]$

9. $90 \div [(82 - 77) \cdot 9]$

10. Find the sum of 2 cubed and 3 squared.

11. Find the difference of 10 squared and 9 squared.

Evaluate the expression when $a = 16$, $b = 8$, and $c = 7$.

12. $8c \div 4$

13. $(c + 5) \div 6$

14. $3a + 2.1(4)$

15. $\dfrac{2a}{15 - c}$

16. $7.2b - bc$

17. $b(a - 9.1)$

18. $ac[(99 - b^2) \cdot 2]$

19. $c^3[4.1(3c - 19)]$

20. $\dfrac{b^3(9 - 5.9)}{3.2(20.4 - 12.4)}$

Practice

For use with pages 16–21

21. The formula to find the area A of a rectangle is $A = \ell w$, where ℓ is the length of the rectangle and w is the width of the rectangle. The figure below can be divided into two rectangles. Find the total area of the figure.

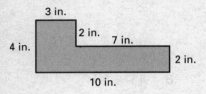

22. You complete a project for your social studies class. There are 3 parts to the project, worth a total of 100 points. You get 50 out of 50 points on part A, and 23 out of 25 points on part C. The total score you received is 93 out of 100. How many points did you get on part B?

23. You use a long distance telephone service that charges $.99 for the first minute of a long distance call and $.10 for each additional minute. Write and evaluate an expression for the total cost of a 17-minute long distance phone call.

Name _____ Date _____

Practice
For use with pages 22–26

Graph the integers on a number line. Then write the integers in order from least to greatest.

1. $-14, -11, -13, -9, -20, -7$

<+—+—+—+—+—+—+—+—+—+—+—+—+>

2. $-30, 20, 10, -15, -5, 35$

<+—+—+—+—+—+—+—+—+—+—+—+—+>

3. $0, -1, 1, -2, 2, -3, 3$

<+—+—+—+—+—+—+—+—+—+—+—+—+>

4. $40, -50, 60, 20, -30, -10$

<+—+—+—+—+—+—+—+—+—+—+—+—+>

Complete the statement using < or >.

5. -9 ____ -17

6. -20 ____ -12

7. 15 ____ -18

8. 0 ____ -24

9. -32 ____ 21

10. 27 ____ -14

State the absolute value of the number.

11. -73

12. -80

13. 16

14. 106

15. -34

16. -54

State the opposite of the number.

17. -98

18. -77

19. 45

20. 70

21. 63

22. -23

Name _____ Date _____

Practice

For use with pages 22–26

Evaluate the expression when $x = -7$.

23. $|-x|$ **24.** $|x| + 4$ **25.** $2|x|$ **26.** $6|x|$

27. $|x| - 5$ **28.** $|x| + 14$ **29.** $-x - 3$ **30.** $-x + 10$

31. The table shows the daily low temperatures recorded over a seven-day period in a town.

Day	Temperature
Sunday	$-10°C$
Monday	$-5°C$
Tuesday	$-11°C$
Wednesday	$-10°C$
Thursday	$-6°C$
Friday	$-7°C$
Saturday	$-9°C$

    a. Did the daily low temperature *increase* or *decrease* from Tuesday to Wednesday?

    b. Did the daily low temperature *increase* or *decrease* from Thursday to Saturday?

    c. Which day's low temperature was lowest? Which was highest?

LESSON
1.5 **Practice**

For use with pages 28–33

Tell whether the sum is positive or negative. You do not need to find the sum.

1. $-27 + (-16)$ **2.** $-18 + 75$

Use a number line to find the sum.

3. $-15 + (-4)$

4. $-21 + (-5)$

5. $-6 + 35$

6. $-42 + 10$

7. $11 + (-47)$

8. $9 + (-53)$

9. $-106 + (-3)$

10. $-94 + (-1)$

11. $81 + (-7)$

Find the sum.

12. $-41 + 30$

13. $-15 + 27$

14. $-21 + (-34)$

15. $-51 + (-23)$

16. $61 + (-33)$

17. $29 + (-48)$

18. $64 + (-17)$

19. $91 + (-26)$

20. $-46 + (-75)$

21. $-9 + 12 + (-4)$

22. $-22 + (-13) + 6$

23. $55 + (-26) + 47$

Name _____ Date _____

Practice
For use with pages 28–33

Evaluate the expression when $a = 8$ and $b = -14$.

24. $a + (-23)$ **25.** $-a + b$ **26.** $-72 + b$

27. $b + 39$ **28.** $a + (-b)$ **29.** $-61 + a$

30. The temperature at 6 A.M. is $-10°$ Fahrenheit. During the day, the temperature rises 6°F, drops 3°F, rises 2°F, and drops 8°F. Write an integer to represent each value. What is the temperature after these changes?

31. The table shows incomes and expenses for a small music store in one week. Write an integer to represent each value. Then find the net profit for the week.

Income		Expense	
Instruments	$800	Displays	$110
Sheet music	$100	Salaries	$400
Lessons	$150		

LESSON
1.6
Practice
For use with pages 34–38

Find the difference.

1. $7 - 11$

2. $15 - 26$

3. $4 - (-20)$

4. $13 - (-8)$

5. $-12 - 9$

6. $-19 - 28$

7. $-2 - (-24)$

8. $-18 - (-5)$

9. $-21 - (-6)$

Evaluate the expression when $x = -14$ and $y = -3$.

10. $x - y$

11. $29 - x$

12. $x - (-17)$

13. $-27 - y$

14. $y - 18$

15. $x - (-23)$

16. $x - 4 - 9$

17. $15 - y - 7$

18. $31 - 35 - y$

Name _____ Date _____

Practice

For use with pages 34–38

Find the change in temperature or elevation.

19. From $-16°C$ to $23°C$

20. From $-47°C$ to $-38°C$

21. From $9°F$ to $-12°F$

22. From $-16°F$ to $-27°F$

23. From -64 meters to -40 meters

24. From -20 meters to 50 meters

25. From 120 yards to -45 yards

26. From -16 feet to -32 feet

27. Find the value of the expression $-9 - (-4) - 6$.

28. Find the value of the expression $102 - (-7) - 270$.

29. A group of hikers on a mountain began at an elevation of 3040 feet above sea level and stopped at an elevation of 2319 feet above sea level. What was their change in elevation between these points? How can you tell from the change in elevation whether the hikers were going up or down the mountain?

30. The temperature at 6 A.M. was 63°F. At 3 P.M., the temperature was 41°F. What was the change in temperature?

Name _____ Date _____

Practice

For use with pages 41–46

Tell whether the product or quotient is *positive* or *negative*. You do not need to find the product or quotient.

1. $16(-23)$

2. $\dfrac{-72}{9}$

3. $-26(-17) \div 13$

Find the product or quotient.

4. $25(-5)$

5. $-29(-4)$

6. $-124 \div 31$

7. $98 \div (-14)$

8. $\dfrac{-102}{-17}$

9. $-32(9)$

10. $-42(-6)$

11. $201 \div (-67)$

12. $-612 \div (-18)$

13. $\dfrac{252}{-4}$

14. $-19(7)$

15. $-21(-11)$

Simplify.

16. $-15(16)(4)$

17. $20(-13)(-32)$

18. $-220 \div 11 \div (-4)$

19. $140 \div (-7) \div (-5)$

20. $24(-8) \div (-6)$

21. $\dfrac{-9(27)}{3}$

Name _____ Date _____

Practice

For use with pages 41–46

Without performing the indicated divisions, complete the statement using >, <, or =.

22. $-642 \div 214$ ____ $-170 \div (-10)$ **23.** $-344 \div (-86)$ ____ $-796 \div 199$

24. Evaluate the expression $\dfrac{5y}{6}$ when $y = 18$.

25. Evaluate the expression $\dfrac{-2m}{9}$ when $m = 27$.

26. The table shows the lowest windchill temperature for each day recorded over two weeks. Find the mean lowest windchill temperature.

Day	Windchill (in °C)	Day	Windchill (in °C)
1	−4	8	−4
2	−5	9	−6
3	−7	10	−2
4	−3	11	−4
5	−3	12	−6
6	−6	13	−10
7	−1	14	−9

Practice

For use with pages 47–51

Give the coordinates of the point.

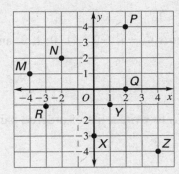

1. X 2. Y

3. Z 4. M

5. N 6. P

7. Q 8. R

Plot the point in a coordinate plane. Describe the location of the point.

9. $(-7, 6)$ 10. $(-5, -3)$ 11. $(2, 3)$

12. $(5, 2)$ 13. $(-4, 0)$ 14. $(3, -6)$

15. $(-2, 1)$ 16. $(5, 0)$ 17. $(0, -2)$

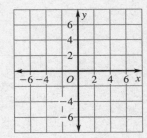

18. Use a coordinate plane.

   a. Plot the points $(0, 0)$, $(0, 4)$, $(5, 4)$, $(8, 2)$, and $(5, 0)$. Connect the points in order. Connect the last point to the first point.

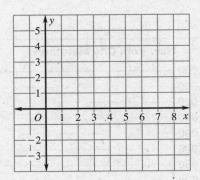

   b. Identify the figure. Explain your reasoning.

Name _____ Date _____

Practice

For use with pages 47–51

19. Use the variable expression $3x - 1$.

    a. Evaluate the expression when $x = -3, -2, -1, 0, 1, 2,$ and 3.

    b. Use your results from part (a) to write a list of ordered pairs in the form $(x, 3x - 1)$.

    c. Plot the ordered pairs $(x, 3x - 1)$ from part (b) in a coordinate plane.

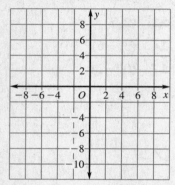

    d. Describe what you notice about the points.

20. The table shows the number of women who finished the New York City Marathon from 1997 to 2001.

Year	1997	1998	1999	2000	2001
Women Finishers	8413	8332	9160	8332	6853

    a. Make a scatter plot of the data.

    b. Describe any relationship you see.

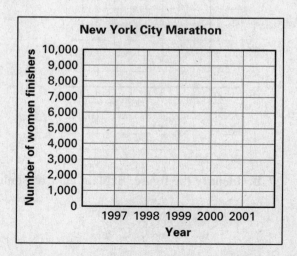

LESSON
2.1 Practice
For use with pages 63–68

Evaluate the expression using mental math. Justify each of your steps.

1. $4(19)(-25)$

2. $17 + 32 + 23$

3. $6.8 + 9.7 + 2.2$

4. $3.06 + 5.37 + 4.94$

5. $10(-8)(-10)(4)$

6. $-15(-9)(4)(5)$

Evaluate the expression when $a = 10$, $b = -4$, and $c = -2$.

7. a^2bc^2

8. $23 \cdot 5c^2$

9. $3bc^2$

10. $a^2b \cdot 6$

11. $9a^2 + 9b \cdot 25$

12. $3b + 5a + (-6c)$

Simplify the expression.

13. $s + 7 + 96$

14. $-33 + j + 14$

15. $-21(3t)$

16. $32r(-6)$

17. $5.36 + p + 6.47$

18. $-2.05x(3.01)$

19. Identify the property illustrated by the statement $(14 \cdot 7) \cdot x = 14 \cdot (7 \cdot x)$.

20. Identify the property illustrated by the statement $18^3 + 0 = 18^3$.

Name _____ Date _____

Practice

For use with pages 63–68

Use a conversion factor to perform the indicated conversion.

21. 27 yards to feet

22. 160 kilometers to meters

23. 540 seconds to minutes

24. 112 ounces to pounds

25. The area of the infield of a college softball field is 3600 square feet. Use a conversion factor to find the area of the infield of a college softball field in square yards.

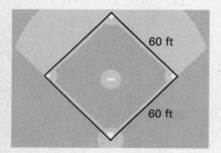

60 ft

60 ft

26. During the summer, you work 5 hours a day as a lifeguard at a beach and earn $8 each hour. Use properties of multiplication to find how much money you earn during a 6-day work week.

27. The cereal box at the right is 14 inches high, 6 inches long, and 2 inches wide. The formula for the volume of a box is $V = \ell wh$. Find the volume of the box in cubic inches.

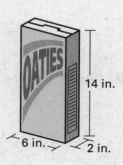

14 in.

6 in.   2 in.

LESSON
2.2

Practice
For use with pages 71–75

Use the distributive property to evaluate the expression.

1. $15(7 + 20)$ **2.** $10(6.4 + 8.9)$ **3.** $-5(24 - 17)$

4. $(4 - 16)(-8)$ **5.** $(29 - 14)(-3)$ **6.** $12(11.3 + 7.8)$

Evaluate the expression using the distributive property and mental math.

7. $312(-4)$ **8.** $487(6)$ **9.** $17.98(3)$

10. $8(1.25)$ **11.** $-7(82)$ **12.** $191(-5)$

Use the distributive property to write an equivalent variable expression.

13. $11(s + 9)$ **14.** $-21(x - 7)$ **15.** $13(20 - a)$

16. $-8(17 + b)$ **17.** $(r + 1.68)(-0.1)$ **18.** $3.25(5.02 - t)$

Name _____   Date _____

Practice

For use with pages 71–75

19. You and a friend go to a restaurant. You each order a salad, a cup of soup, and a drink. Each salad costs $5.99, each cup of soup costs $3.90, and each drink costs $1.15. Use the distributive property to find the total cost of the meal.

20. There are several rectangular parcels of land for sale in a neighborhood. The Gonzalez family wants to purchase Lot A and half of the neighboring lot.

   a. Use the distributive property to find the area, in square yards, of Lot A.

   b. Use the distributive property to find the area, in square yards, of half of Lot B.

   c. Find the total area of the land the Gonzalez family wishes to purchase.

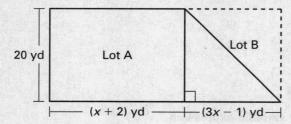

Find the area of the rectangle or triangle.

21.

24m + 1
8

22.
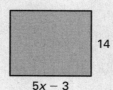
14
5x − 3

23.
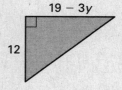
19 − 3y
12

Name _____ Date _____

Practice

For use with pages 78–83

1. Describe and correct the error in the solution.

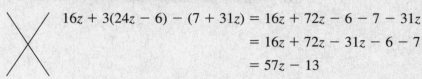

$$16z + 3(24z - 6) - (7 + 31z) = 16z + 72z - 6 - 7 - 31z$$
$$= 16z + 72z - 31z - 6 - 7$$
$$= 57z - 13$$

For the given expression, identify the terms, like terms, coefficients, and constant terms. Then simplify the expression.

2. $4d - 5 - 9d + 17$

3. $-8p - 12 + 7p - 11$

4. $27 - 13t + 32 - 2t + 10t$

5. $6f - 14 + 26 - 3f - 15f$

6. $-11j + 16 - 22j - 27 + 5j$

7. $-18 + 3z + 23 - 19z + 7z$

Simplify the expression.

8. $-4(5c + 7) - 3c + 13$

9. $-11(9 - 3y) + 12y - 14$

10. $2(3a - 6) - 15a - 26$

11. $-(19 - 2g^2) - 57 + 4g^2$

12. $24u - 6(8 - 4u) + 52$

13. $16x^2 - 5(7 - x^2) + 43$

14. $-(21k - 3 + 4) - 17k$

15. $8(6h - 11) + 5(20 - 3h)$

16. $10(7 - 4b) - 9(21b - 8)$

Name _____ Date _____

Practice

For use with pages 78–83

17. $-m^2 + 14 - (6m^2 + 13 + m^2)$ **18.** $-5w^2 + 23 - (29 - 4w^2 + 9)$

19. $28 - 6n + 7(2n - 8) - 3n$ **20.** $21 - 7(19 - x^2 + 6) - 3x^2 + 1$

21. You are making a rectangular poster to advertise a school fundraiser. You want the poster to be twice as long as it is wide. Let w represent the width (in meters) of the poster.

  a. Write and simplify an expression in terms of w for the perimeter of the poster.

  b. Write and simplify an expression in terms of w for the area of the poster.

  c. Complete the table.

Width (meters)	1	2	3	4
Perimeter (meters)				
Area (square meters)				

  d. Which width given in the table allows for the most area while not exceeding a perimeter of 20 meters?

Write and simplify an expression for the perimeter of the triangle or rectangle.

22.
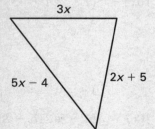
3x
5x − 4   2x + 5

23.
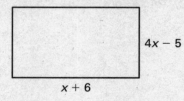
4x − 5
x + 6

24.
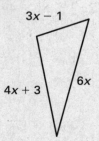
3x − 1
4x + 3   6x

<table>
<tr><td>LESSON</td></tr>
<tr><td>2.4</td></tr>
</table>

Practice

For use with pages 85–89

Write the verbal sentence as an equation.

1. The difference of 11 and y is -9.

2. The sum of 41 and w is 26.

3. The quotient of r and 6 is -4.

4. The product of 18 and p is 54.

Tell whether the given value of the variable is a solution of the equation.

5. $\frac{v}{-4} = 13; v = -52$

6. $108 = -36z; z = -3$

7. $27 = n - 16; n = 11$

8. $84 = 78 + t; t = -6$

Match the equation with the corresponding question. Then solve.

9. $\frac{a}{2} = 36$

    A. What number minus 36 equals 2?

    B. What number divided by 2 equals 36?

    C. 2 times what number equals 36?

    D. 2 plus what number equals 36?

10. $2a = 36$

11. $2 + a = 36$

12. $a - 36 = 2$

Name _____   Date _____

Practice
For use with pages 85–89

Solve the equation using mental math.

13. $12b = -108$

14. $96 = -8m$

15. $49 = 7d$

16. $\dfrac{w}{-3} = 21$

17. $\dfrac{48}{h} = -16$

18. $-8 = \dfrac{k}{-4}$

19. $39 - f = 15$

20. $58 = 27 - \ell$

21. $z - 41 = 63$

22. $y + 43 = 58$

23. $-19 + c = 28$

24. $g + 26 = -61$

In Exercises 25 and 26, use an equation to solve the problem.

25. While traveling a long distance, an elephant in a family walks at a rate of about 10 miles per hour. Find the approximate time it takes an elephant to travel 60 miles.

26. From 2003 to 2004, the number of students in a school declined by 140 students. In 2004, there were 530 students in the school. Find the number of students in the school in 2003.

27. The perimeter of the figure is 48 centimeters.

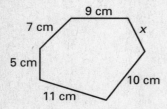

a. Write and simplify an equation that you can use to find x.

b. Solve your equation. What is the value of x?

Name _____ Date _____

Practice
For use with pages 102–107

Perform the indicated operation.

1. $-7.06 + 5.22$

2. $-8.17 + (-12.91)$

3. $13.07 - 20.01$

4. $-6.47 - 10.16$

5. $-15.23 - (-9.57)$

6. $-4.34 - 11.59$

7. $-16.04(-5.25)$

8. $-21.9(14.8)$

9. $18.05(-3.12)$

10. $42.125 \div -6.74$

11. $-96.38 \div -12.2$

12. $-42.822 \div 14.04$

Solve the equation. Check your solution.

13. $21.3 + r = -19.79$

14. $13.49 = -8.56 + a$

15. $-20.57 = m + 3.78$

16. $v - 17.06 = 29.08$

17. $-14.88 = d - 34.76$

18. $-31.45 = p - 12.96$

19. $30.75b = -73.8$

20. $70.448 = -25.16f$

21. $-42.12 = -7.8t$

22. $-13.25 = \dfrac{k}{-6}$

23. $24.36 = \dfrac{w}{-7.9}$

24. $\dfrac{c}{-20.18} = -7.35$

Name _____   Date _____

Practice

For use with pages 102–107

25. You deposit a check for $236.79 into your savings account. Your account
has a balance of $319.23 after the deposit. Find the balance of your savings
account before the deposit.

26. The table shows the daily low temperature in degrees Celsius for a
5-day period.

Day	Monday	Tuesday	Wednesday	Thursday	Friday
Temperature (°C)	−5.24	−8.3	−9.47	−9.08	−5.13

    a. Find the sum of the temperatures.

    b. Find the average low temperature for the 5-day period.

Simplify the expression.

27. $-9.87x - 18.13x$ **28.** $27.33x - 39.42x$ **29.** $-56.08x + 26.68x$

Find the value of x for the given triangle or rectangle.

30. Perimeter = 50.35 m   **31.** Perimeter = 24.31 ft   **32.** Area = 49.65 cm^2

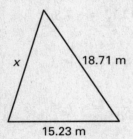

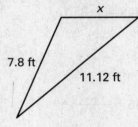

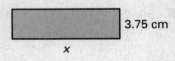

Name _____ Date _____

Practice

For use with pages 119–124

Tell whether the given value of the variable is a solution of the equation.

1. $6x - 7 = 17; x = 4$ **2.** $1 = 4x + 9; x = -2$ **3.** $8 - 3x = 5; x = -1$

4. $-15 = -3x + 15; x = 5$ **5.** $\frac{x}{5} - 6 = -2; x = 20$ **6.** $-6 = \frac{x}{2} - 7; x = -2$

Solve the equation. Check your solution.

7. $7x + 12 = 26$ **8.** $2x + 9 = -5$ **9.** $-4 = 9x + 23$

10. $-10 = 6x - 16$ **11.** $25 - 3x = -8$ **12.** $4x - 15 = 25$

13. $70 = 19 - 3x$ **14.** $-2x - 47 = -11$ **15.** $-14 = -22 - \frac{x}{3}$

16. $\frac{x}{12} + 13 = 18$ **17.** $-10 = 8 - \frac{x}{7}$ **18.** $3 = \frac{x}{25} + 6$

19. $250 = 124 - 3x$ **20.** $-\frac{x}{9} - 12 = -23$ **21.** $56 - \frac{x}{15} = 47$

Name _____ Date _____

Practice

For use with pages 119–124

Write the verbal sentence as an equation. Then solve the equation.

22. Fourteen minus the product of 3 and a number is 26.

23. Negative seven minus the product of 5 and number is 28.

24. Eleven minus the quotient of a number and 8 is 15.

25. Negative sixteen plus the quotient of a number and 2 is 35.

26. Thirty-nine minus a number is -19.

27. Fifteen people volunteer for a park cleanup. The number of volunteers increases by 7 people each month for several months. After how many months will there be 50 volunteers?

28. You have a $100 gift card to spend at a store. You buy a portable compact disc player for $45. Compact discs are on sale for $11 each. How many compact discs can you buy with the money remaining on the gift card?

29. A group of 4 friends are playing golf. The total cost of the round of golf is $108. Each person in the group has the same coupon. The total cost of the round with the coupons is $76. How much is the coupon worth?

30. A school makes $715 from ticket sales for a school play. From the ticket sales, $448 is from adult tickets. Student tickets are $3 each. How many students attended the play?

31. You are rock climbing and descending a cliff at a rate of about 9 feet per minute. The cliff is about 360 feet high.

   a. How long until you are at a height of 234 feet?

   b. How long until you are halfway down the cliff?

Name _____ Date _____

Practice

For use with pages 138–142

Tell whether the given number is a solution of $-8 > -17 + x - 14$.

1. -23　　　　**2.** 23　　　　**3.** 0　　　　**4.** 25

Write an inequality that represents the verbal sentence.

5. Nine and four tenths plus a number is less than or equal to 14.1.

6. Thirty two plus a number minus 18 is greater than -3.

7. Six tenths plus 4.7 plus a number is greater than or equal to -5.6.

8. A number minus 6.88 is less than 22.74.

Match the inequality with the graph of its solution.

A.
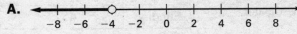

B.
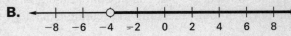

C.
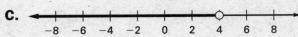

D.
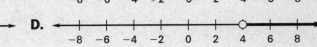

9. $x - 8 - 11 < -15$

10. $13 > -6 + 23 + x$

11. $10.45 + x - 5 > 1.45$

12. $4.5 + x - 4 > 4.5$

LESSON
3.4
Continued

Practice

For use with pages 138–142

Solve the inequality. Graph your solution.

13. $7 + x + 10 < -2$

$\leftarrow\!\!+\!\!+\!\!+\!\!+\!\!+\!\!+\!\!+\!\!+\!\!+\!\!+\!\!+\!\!\rightarrow$

14. $5 + x - 9 \geq 4$

$\leftarrow\!\!+\!\!+\!\!+\!\!+\!\!+\!\!+\!\!+\!\!+\!\!+\!\!+\!\!+\!\!\rightarrow$

15. $x - 12 - 14 \leq 6$

$\leftarrow\!\!+\!\!+\!\!+\!\!+\!\!+\!\!+\!\!+\!\!+\!\!+\!\!+\!\!+\!\!\rightarrow$

16. $-7 - 15 + x > -15$

$\leftarrow\!\!+\!\!+\!\!+\!\!+\!\!+\!\!+\!\!+\!\!+\!\!+\!\!+\!\!+\!\!\rightarrow$

17. $-23 \leq x - 18 + 25$

$\leftarrow\!\!+\!\!+\!\!+\!\!+\!\!+\!\!+\!\!+\!\!+\!\!+\!\!+\!\!+\!\!\rightarrow$

18. $2.9 + x + 7.5 > 6$

$\leftarrow\!\!+\!\!+\!\!+\!\!+\!\!+\!\!+\!\!+\!\!+\!\!+\!\!+\!\!+\!\!\rightarrow$

19. $-12.1 + 16.4 + x < -3.7$

$\leftarrow\!\!+\!\!+\!\!+\!\!+\!\!+\!\!+\!\!+\!\!+\!\!+\!\!+\!\!+\!\!\rightarrow$

20. $-2.87 - 4.66 + x > -7.53$

$\leftarrow\!\!+\!\!+\!\!+\!\!+\!\!+\!\!+\!\!+\!\!+\!\!+\!\!+\!\!+\!\!\rightarrow$

21. $-1.12 \leq x + 1.53 - 4.01$

$\leftarrow\!\!+\!\!+\!\!+\!\!+\!\!+\!\!+\!\!+\!\!+\!\!+\!\!+\!\!+\!\!\rightarrow$

22. $10 + 11.88 + x \leq -4.5$

$\leftarrow\!\!+\!\!+\!\!+\!\!+\!\!+\!\!+\!\!+\!\!+\!\!+\!\!+\!\!+\!\!\rightarrow$

23. $42.76 - 21.15 \geq x + 12.9$

$\leftarrow\!\!+\!\!+\!\!+\!\!+\!\!+\!\!+\!\!+\!\!+\!\!+\!\!+\!\!+\!\!\rightarrow$

24. $-140.67 < 74.9 - 101.23 + x$

$\leftarrow\!\!+\!\!+\!\!+\!\!+\!\!+\!\!+\!\!+\!\!+\!\!+\!\!+\!\!+\!\!\rightarrow$

25. The table shows the number of preordered tickets for a three-day showing of a play. The theater has a seating capacity of 5400 people. Write and solve an inequality that represents the possible number of tickets t that can be sold at the door for each night of the play without exceeding the seating capacity of the theater.

Night	Preorder tickets
Friday	3488
Saturday	4109
Sunday	4573

26. An elevator has a weight limit of 2000 pounds. The weights in pounds of twelve people on the elevator are shown below.

175, 140, 135, 155, 170, 190, 125, 160, 150, 150, 130, 145

a. Find the total weight of the twelve people on the elevator.

b. A thirteenth person wants to get on the elevator. Write and solve an inequality that represents the weight w that person can be without exceeding the elevator's weight limit.

LESSON
3.5 **Practice**
For use with pages 143–148

Tell whether the given number is a solution of $-1.5x > -12$.

1. -4 **2.** 12 **3.** 0 **4.** 8

Match the inequality with the graph of its solution.

5. $\dfrac{x}{1.4} > -10$ **A.**

6. $-3.5x > 14$ **B.**

7. $\dfrac{x}{-1.4} > 10$ **C.**

8. $-3.5x < 14$ **D.**

Solve the inequality. Graph your solution.

9. $\dfrac{x}{-10} \le 22$

10. $\dfrac{x}{25} > -30$

11. $-13x < -208$

12. $45x \le -855$

13. $1.6x \le -11.2$

14. $-5.3x > 21.2$

15. $-10.7 > \dfrac{x}{-4}$

16. $8.3 \le \dfrac{x}{-5}$

17. $\dfrac{x}{1.3} \ge 7.1$

18. $\dfrac{x}{-5.6} < 2.8$

Name _____ Date _____

Practice

For use with pages 143–148

19. $-3.8x \geq 28.5$

20. $10.4x > 520$

21. $-0.1x \leq -2.5$

22. $-9.8x \geq 44.1$

23. $\dfrac{x}{-12.7} \geq -2.2$

24. $\dfrac{x}{4.2} < -20.45$

Write the verbal sentence as an inequality. Then solve the inequality.

25. A number divided by 3.5 is greater than or equal to 7.8.

26. The product of a number and -5 is less than -1.6.

27. The product of a number and -0.9 is greater than 27.

28. A number divided by -4.75 is greater than or equal to -20.

29. You need to complete at least 300 math problems in 4 days for a homework assignment. How many exercises should you complete each day?

30. An admission pass for an art museum is $4.50. Write and solve an inequality to find the number of passes p that must be sold for the museum to make at least $7200.

Name _____ Date _____

Practice

For use with pages 149–153

Tell whether the given number is a solution of $2(3x + 1) \geq 7x + 4$.

1. -1 **2.** -2 **3.** -10 **4.** 0

Match the inequality with the graph of its solution.

5. $3(4x - 1) \leq 10x + 25$

A.

```
←——+——+——+——●——+——+——+——→
  -16  -15  -14  -13  -12  -11
```

B.

```
←——+——+——●————————————————→
   12   13   14   15   16   17
```

6. $2(14 - 3x) \leq -4x$

C.

```
←————————————●——+——+——+——→
  -16  -15  -14  -13  -12  -11
```

D.

```
←——————————————●——+——+——+——→
   12   13   14   15   16   17
```

7. $-7x + 17 \geq 115$

8. $\dfrac{x + 4}{5} \geq -2$

Solve the inequality. Graph your solution.

9. $-6x - 15 > 57$

```
←—+——+——+——+——+——+——→
```

10. $22 > \dfrac{x}{-12} + 4$

```
←—+——+——+——+——+——+——→
```

11. $-3(2 - x) \leq 2x - 9$

```
←—+——+——+——+——+——+——→
```

12. $6(5 - 2x) < 5x + 13$

```
←—+——+——+——+——+——+——→
```

13. $\dfrac{3x - 1}{4} < 8$

```
←—+——+——+——+——+——+——→
```

14. $\dfrac{2x + 5}{3} \geq -7$

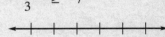

LESSON
3.6 **Practice**
Continued | For use with pages 149–153

15. $\dfrac{-x-11}{3} \leq 21$

16. $-8 < \dfrac{5x+4}{7}$

17. $4x + 22 > -2(14 + 3x)$

18. $-4(x + 10) \geq -7x + 65$

19. $8(3x - 19) < 15x + 73$

20. $74 < \dfrac{-17x+30}{5}$

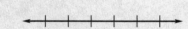

21. $\dfrac{25x-41}{13} \leq 18$

22. $12(2x - 13) > 117 - 15x$

23. $29x - 515 \leq -14(8 - 3x)$

24. The golf course you play at charges $22 per round of golf. You can either rent golf clubs at the course for $8 or you can buy your own set of clubs for $160. Write and solve an inequality to find the number of rounds of golf you need to play in order for the cost of purchasing clubs to be less than the cost of renting clubs. Let r represent the number of rounds of golf.

25. For what values of x is the area of the rectangle shown greater than 100 square units?

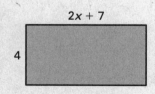

26. For what values of x is the perimeter of the rectangle shown greater than 50 units?

42 **Pre-Algebra**
Chapter 3   Practice Workbook

LESSON
4.1

Practice

For use with pages 171–176

Write all the factors of the number.

1. 28

2. 34

3. 44

4. 46

5. 59

6. 65

Tell whether the number is *prime* or *composite*.

7. 97

8. 127

9. 111

10. 99

11. 133

12. 149

Complete the factor tree. Then write the prime factorization of the number.

13.

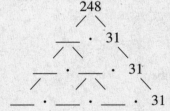

14.

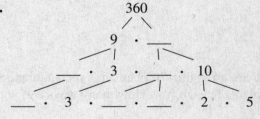

Name _____ Date _____

Practice

For use with pages 171–176

Write the prime factorization of the number.

15. 56   **16.** 69   **17.** 57

18. 77   **19.** 91   **20.** 85

21. 93   **22.** 114   **23.** 108

Factor the monomial.

24. $16x^2y$ **25.** $32b^5c^4$ **26.** $17r^2s^3$

27. $24z^2$ **28.** $40g^3h$ **29.** $57cd^4$

30. Exercise 14 shows a factor tree for 360. Make another factor tree for 360, without using 9 as a factor in the first part of the tree. Compare the results of the trees.

31. You are arranging 70 plants in a rectangular garden with the same number of plants in each row. How many ways can you arrange the garden?

32. A dog kennel groups the dogs in order to determine at what time they will be given a treat. Each group should have the same number of dogs. There are 120 dogs in the kennel. How many groups are possible?

LESSON
4.2

Practice

For use with pages 177–181

Find the greatest common factor of the numbers.

1. 24, 60

2. 28, 70

3. 48, 80

4. 66, 71

5. 25, 42

6. 63, 49

Find the greatest common factor of the numbers. Then tell whether the numbers are relatively prime.

7. 22, 64

8. 26, 65

9. 44, 47

10. 36, 48

11. 51, 68

12. 11, 98

Find the greatest common factor of the monomials.

13. $14m^2, 21m$

14. $34n, 8n^2$

15. $16t^3, 24t^2$

16. $6x, 9x^2, 18x^3$

17. $24y^2, 6y^2, 8y$

18. $15a, 45a^2, 35a^4$

Tell whether the numbers are relatively prime.

19. 210, 211

20. 62, 121

21. 81, 87

Name _____ Date _____

Practice

For use with pages 177–181

Find the greatest common factor of the monomials.

22. $32xy, 20y^2$

23. $33pq, 55p^2q^2$

24. $16abc^2, 28abc$

25. $52d^2e, 12d^2f$

26. $12rst, 42r^2s^3t^2, rt^5$

27. $9xy^2z, 18y^3, 6x$

28. A baseball league forms using a total of 12 coaches, 78 players, 24 baseball bats, and 96 baseballs. What is the greatest number of teams that can be formed that have equal numbers of coaches, players, baseball bats, and baseballs?

29. A food drive takes in a total of 63 cans of soup, 45 loaves of bread, 72 cans of spaghetti sauce, and 36 boxes of spaghetti. What is the greatest number of identical care packages that can be put together from the items obtained?

30. Two numbers are relatively prime. If the first number is multiplied by 3, the result is divisible by 6. Can the second number be an odd number? Explain your reasoning.

LESSON 4.3 Practice

For use with pages 182–186

Tell whether the fraction is in simplest form.

1. $\frac{13}{39}$

2. $\frac{25}{42}$

3. $\frac{15}{51}$

Write two fractions that are equivalent to the given fraction.

4. $\frac{5}{14}$

5. $\frac{7}{16}$

6. $\frac{18}{20}$

7. $\frac{22}{34}$

8. $\frac{14}{35}$

9. $\frac{12}{46}$

Write the fraction in simplest form.

10. $\frac{21}{24}$

11. $\frac{28}{30}$

12. $\frac{39}{52}$

13. $\frac{45}{72}$

14. $\frac{35}{42}$

15. $\frac{14}{63}$

16. You spend 3 hours every day practicing the piano. What fraction of a day do you spend practicing the piano? Give your answer in simplest form.

Name _____ Date _____

Practice

For use with pages 182–186

17. You and a friend are taking a 300-mile car trip. You have already traveled 120 miles.

  a. What fraction of the trip has been completed? Give your answer in simplest form.

  b. What fraction of the trip is left? Give your answer in simplest form.

Write the fraction in simplest form.

18. $\dfrac{60x^3y}{40x^2y^2}$

19. $\dfrac{135mn^4}{50n^2}$

20. $\dfrac{28s}{35s^2t^3}$

21. $\dfrac{63v^4r}{25r^2}$

22. $\dfrac{75a^3b}{245ab^3}$

23. $\dfrac{28g^3h}{56g^3h^2}$

Use a number line to determine whether the fractions are equivalent.

24. $\dfrac{3}{8}, \dfrac{8}{24}$

25. $\dfrac{1}{7}, \dfrac{8}{14}$

26. $\dfrac{4}{5}, \dfrac{16}{20}$

Write the fractions in simplest form. Tell whether they are equivalent.

27. $\dfrac{39}{72}, \dfrac{26}{48}$

28. $\dfrac{42}{56}, \dfrac{63}{84}$

29. $\dfrac{68}{102}, \dfrac{80}{96}$

Name _____ Date _____

Practice
For use with pages 187–191

Find the least common multiple of the numbers.

1. 24, 28

2. 20, 36

3. 42, 63

4. 5, 10, 15

5. 9, 12, 16

6. 14, 21, 35

Find the least common multiple of the monomials.

7. $13b^3$, $7b^2$

8. $8y$, $18y^3$

9. $24a$, $32a^4$

10. $31z^3$, $93z^2$

11. $21m^2n$, $84mn^3$

12. $50s^3t^2$, $60st$

Use the LCD to determine which fraction is greater.

13. $\frac{13}{18}$, $\frac{16}{21}$

14. $\frac{17}{30}$, $\frac{27}{35}$

15. $\frac{19}{34}$, $\frac{19}{36}$

16. $\frac{31}{52}$, $\frac{37}{64}$

17. $\frac{9}{20}$, $\frac{19}{46}$

18. $\frac{15}{34}$, $\frac{29}{51}$

Name _____ Date _____

Practice

For use with pages 187–191

19. You have dance class every 3 days. Today is Monday, and you have dance class. In how many more days will you have dance class on Monday again? Use the LCM to find your answer. Then check your answer using the calendar shown. On what date will you have dance class on Monday again?

August						
S	M	Tu	W	Th	F	S
	①	2	3	4	5	6
7	8	9	10	11	12	13
14	15	16	17	18	19	20
21	22	23	24	25	26	27
28	29	30	31			

20. Ginny has two vegetable gardens. In the first garden, Ginny grows tomatoes every 2 years. In the second garden, Ginny grows tomatoes every 3 years. This year, Ginny grows tomatoes in both gardens. In how many years will she grow tomatoes in both gardens again?

Order the numbers from least to greatest.

21. $\dfrac{19}{6}, 3\dfrac{5}{14}, \dfrac{83}{21}$

22. $\dfrac{71}{9}, \dfrac{239}{33}, 7\dfrac{2}{3}$

23. $\dfrac{11}{4}, 2\dfrac{16}{17}, \dfrac{99}{34}$

24. $\dfrac{47}{8}, \dfrac{303}{56}, 5\dfrac{25}{28}$

25. $3\dfrac{1}{6}, \dfrac{139}{45}, \dfrac{55}{18}$

26. $\dfrac{61}{48}, 1\dfrac{5}{16}, \dfrac{31}{24}$

Rewrite the variable expressions with a common denominator.

27. $\dfrac{c}{8}, \dfrac{c}{14}$

28. $\dfrac{3a}{4b}, \dfrac{b}{10a}$

29. $\dfrac{4t}{9w^2}, \dfrac{5}{6wt}$

Name _____ Date _____

Practice
For use with pages 193–198

Find the product or quotient. Write your answer using exponents.

1. $5^{10} \cdot 5^{11}$

2. $4^8 \cdot 4^9$

3. $6^7 \cdot 6^2 \cdot 6^8$

4. $8^2 \cdot 8^{14} \cdot 8^3$

5. $9^{12} \cdot 9^{13}$

6. $10^7 \cdot 10^{13}$

7. $\dfrac{3^{16}}{3^8}$

8. $\dfrac{7^{20}}{7^{14}}$

9. $\dfrac{11^{19}}{11^{15}}$

10. $\dfrac{13^5}{13^2}$

11. $\dfrac{16^8}{16^5}$

12. $\dfrac{20^9}{20^7}$

Simplify.

13. $d^4 \cdot d^4$

14. $3h^5 \cdot 4h^6$

15. $5g^2 \cdot g^{16}$

16. $8e^9 \cdot 7e^{10}$

17. $9w^3 \cdot 2w^4 \cdot w^2$

18. $5v^6 \cdot 2v^4 \cdot 2v^3$

19. $\dfrac{x^{15}}{x^9}$

20. $\dfrac{9y^{18}}{15y^2}$

21. $\dfrac{12s^9}{32s^2}$

22. $\dfrac{15z^{11}}{18z^7}$

23. $\dfrac{30a^5 \cdot a^3}{12a}$

24. $\dfrac{6h^{11} \cdot 7h^6}{28h^3}$

Name _____   Date _____

Practice

For use with pages 193–198

Find the area of the rectangle.

25.

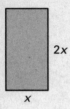

2x

x

26.

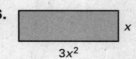

x

$3x^2$

27.

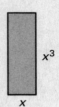

x^3

x

28. A file on the hard drive of a computer is 3^2 kilobytes. Another file is 3^7 kilobytes. How many times larger is the second file than the first file? Write your answer using an exponent.

Find the missing exponent.

29. $u^{22} \cdot u^{18} = u^?$

30. $d^? \cdot d^{13} = d^{24}$

31. $f^8 \cdot f^? = f^{33}$

32. $\dfrac{x^{29}}{x^9} = x^?$

33. $\dfrac{m^?}{m^9} = m^{15}$

34. $\dfrac{r^{31}}{r^?} = r^{17}$

LESSON
4.6 **Practice**
For use with pages 199–203

Name _____ Date _____

1. Which expression is *not* equivalent to $x^3 \cdot x^{-7}$?

A. x^{-4} **B.** $\dfrac{1}{x^4}$ **C.** $\dfrac{x^7}{x^3}$ **D.** $\dfrac{x^3}{x^7}$

Write the expression using only positive exponents.

2. 14^{-3}

3. 9^{-7}

4. 18^{-5}

5. ab^0

6. $24d^{-1}$

7. $m^4 n^{-2}$

Write the expression without using a fraction bar.

8. $\dfrac{1}{27}$

9. $\dfrac{1}{81}$

10. $\dfrac{1}{63}$

11. $\dfrac{5}{t^4}$

12. $\dfrac{6z}{y^5}$

13. $\dfrac{11p^2}{q^6}$

Find the product. Write your answer using only positive exponents.

14. $22^0 \cdot 22^4$

15. $8^5 \cdot 8^{-6}$

16. $12^{-4} \cdot 12^{-7}$

17. $3w^{-9} \cdot w^4$

18. $9h^{-2} \cdot 5h^{10}$

19. $14m^{-4} \cdot 6m^{-9}$

Name _____ Date _____

Practice

For use with pages 199–203

20. Scientists have created a 10-nanometer transistor for use in computers. A nanometer is 10^{-9} meter. What is the length of the transistor in meters?

21. Write the number $\dfrac{1}{10,000,000}$ as a power of 10 using a negative exponent.

22. A milligram is 10^{-3} gram. A kilogram is 10^3 grams. How many times the mass of a milligram is the mass of a kilogram?

Find the quotient. Write your answer using only positive exponents.

23. $\dfrac{18a^{-20}}{8a^9}$

24. $\dfrac{30u^{-15}}{34u^{-16}}$

25. $\dfrac{19k^{-10}}{k^{16}}$

26. $\dfrac{14r^3}{r^{-8}}$

27. $\dfrac{c^{10}d^0}{c^9d^5}$

28. $\dfrac{w^3y^{13}}{w^{11}y^6}$

Use a calculator to evaluate the expression. If necessary, round the result to the nearest thousandth.

29. $(6.5)^{-3}$

30. $(9.4)^{-3}$

31. $(7.4)^{-2}$

Name _____   Date _____

Practice

For use with pages 204–209

Write the number in scientific notation.

1. 1250

2. 205,000

3. 0.0035

4. 0.00058

5. 5,220,000

6. 0.000064

Write the number in standard form.

7. 5.3×10^2

8. 7.2×10^{-2}

9. 4.3×10^{-3}

10. 1.2×10^5

11. 9.45×10^{-5}

12. 6.32×10^6

Complete the statement using <, >, or =.

13. 1.8×10^2 _____ 1800

14. 43,000 _____ 4.3×10^3

15. 6.9×10^{-3} _____ 0.0068

16. 1.8×10^{-4} _____ 0.0018

Find the product. Write your answer in scientific notation.

17. $(6 \times 10^2)(3 \times 10^3)$

18. $(4.5 \times 10^3)(2 \times 10^4)$

19. $(4 \times 10^{-3})(2.4 \times 10^7)$

20. $(2.5 \times 10^{-2})(5 \times 10^{-3})$

Name _____   Date _____

Practice
For use with pages 204–209

21. The sun has a diameter of 1.39×10^6 kilometers. The diameter of Earth is 1.28×10^4 kilometers. How many times larger is the sun's diameter than the Earth's diameter? Give your answer in scientific notation.

Order the numbers from least to greatest.

22. $2400; 2.5 \times 10^2; 2.3 \times 10^3$

23. $4.8 \times 10^5; 481,000; 4.7 \times 10^5$

24. $0.036; 3.5 \times 10^{-2}; 3.7 \times 10^{-2}$

25. $8.3 \times 10^{-4}; 0.0084; 8.2 \times 10^{-4}$

Write the number in scientific notation.

26. Volume (in cubic kilometers) of water in Lake Michigan: 4920

27. Approximate density (in grams per milliliter) of one helium atom: 0.0001787

Write the number in standard form.

28. Floor area (in square meters) of the Sears Tower in Chicago: 4.16×10^5

29. Approximate width (in meters) of a United States dollar bill: 6.6294×10^{-2}

30. Volume (in cubic meters) of a mole of helium atoms: 2.1×10^{-5}

LESSON
5.1 Practice

For use with pages 219–224

Show that the number is rational by writing it as a quotient of two integers.

1. 273

2. −86

3. $6\frac{9}{10}$

4. $-9\frac{1}{12}$

5. 3400

6. −555

7. $-2\frac{7}{20}$

8. $4\frac{11}{14}$

Write the fraction or mixed number as a decimal.

9. $\frac{8}{25}$

10. $-\frac{5}{18}$

11. $-3\frac{2}{11}$

12. $8\frac{3}{20}$

13. $\frac{34}{3}$

14. $-\frac{29}{4}$

15. $6\frac{37}{100}$

16. $-2\frac{9}{40}$

17. $-\frac{7}{18}$

18. $\frac{39}{26}$

19. $5\frac{14}{15}$

20. $-10\frac{7}{36}$

Write the decimal as a fraction or mixed number.

21. 0.65

22. 0.04

23. −5.28

24. 14.005

25. $-8.\overline{4}$

26. $0.\overline{16}$

27. $-0.1\overline{3}$

28. $3.7\overline{6}$

Name _____ Date _____

Practice
For use with pages 219–224

Order the numbers from least to greatest.

29. $-\dfrac{6}{11}, -0.55, -0.\overline{5}, -\dfrac{27}{50}$

30. $0.69, \dfrac{13}{20}, \dfrac{1}{2}, 0.6, \dfrac{17}{25}$

31. $-1.5, -\dfrac{7}{4}, -\dfrac{8}{5}, -1.7, -0.\overline{8}, -\dfrac{11}{6}$

32. $4.41, \dfrac{43}{10}, 4.1, 4.02, \dfrac{17}{4}, 4\dfrac{1}{5}$

33. On Monday, a deli takes 250 orders. Of these, 144 are carry-out orders. On Tuesday, it takes 220 orders. Of these, 125 are carry-out orders. Which day has the greater fraction of carry-out orders?

In Exercises 34–36, use the table that shows the results of a survey about the kind of fruit that students like best.

Favorite fruit	Orange	Banana	Pear	Strawberry	Apple
Portion of students	$\dfrac{7}{25}$	$\dfrac{2}{5}$	$\dfrac{7}{100}$	$\dfrac{1}{12}$	$\dfrac{1}{6}$

34. Write each fraction as a decimal. Tell whether the decimal form of the fraction is repeating or terminating.

35. Which fruit was chosen most often?

36. Is it easier to compare the survey results in fraction form or decimal form? Explain.

Name _____ Date _____

Practice

For use with pages 225–229

Find the sum or difference.

1. $\dfrac{12}{13} + \dfrac{12}{13}$

2. $\dfrac{1}{10} - \dfrac{9}{10}$

3. $-\dfrac{13}{32} + \left(-\dfrac{13}{32}\right)$

4. $\dfrac{34}{43} - \left(-\dfrac{12}{43}\right)$

5. $-\dfrac{11}{30} - \left(-\dfrac{7}{30}\right)$

6. $-\dfrac{17}{50} + \dfrac{19}{50}$

7. $\dfrac{43}{100} - \left(-\dfrac{17}{100}\right)$

8. $\dfrac{9}{80} - \dfrac{51}{80}$

9. $8\dfrac{7}{10} + 3\dfrac{9}{10}$

10. $5\dfrac{1}{7} - 6\dfrac{2}{7}$

11. $3\dfrac{1}{15} - 7\dfrac{11}{15}$

12. $1\dfrac{2}{9} - 12\dfrac{7}{9}$

13. $24\dfrac{17}{22} - 16\dfrac{5}{22}$

14. $\dfrac{4}{5} - \left(-3\dfrac{4}{5}\right)$

15. $20\dfrac{5}{6} + \left(-18\dfrac{5}{6}\right)$

16. $-4\dfrac{11}{16} - \dfrac{15}{16}$

Simplify the expression.

17. $\dfrac{7x}{20} + \dfrac{17x}{20}$

18. $\dfrac{19x}{28} + \dfrac{x}{28}$

19. $-\dfrac{9}{14x} + \dfrac{17}{14x}$

20. $-\dfrac{4x}{45} - \dfrac{41x}{45}$

21. $\dfrac{4}{x} - \dfrac{11}{x}$

22. $\dfrac{7}{24x} + \left(-\dfrac{5}{24x}\right)$

23. $\dfrac{11}{12x} - \left(-\dfrac{5}{12x}\right)$

24. $\dfrac{8}{5x} + \dfrac{3}{5x} - \left(-\dfrac{4}{5x}\right)$

Name _____ Date _____

Practice

For use with pages 225–229

Evaluate the expression.

25. $\dfrac{1}{12} + \dfrac{5}{12} + \dfrac{11}{12}$

26. $\dfrac{5}{8} + \dfrac{7}{8} + \left(-\dfrac{3}{8}\right)$

27. $-\dfrac{9}{14} + \dfrac{3}{14} + \dfrac{5}{14}$

28. $\dfrac{4}{7} - \left(-\dfrac{2}{7}\right) + \dfrac{5}{7}$

29. $-\dfrac{7}{9} - \dfrac{4}{9} - \dfrac{2}{9}$

30. $-\dfrac{9}{20} + \dfrac{11}{20} - \left(-\dfrac{3}{20}\right)$

31. You have a piece of wood that is $7\dfrac{3}{4}$ feet long. You want to cut one piece that is $3\dfrac{7}{12}$ feet long and one piece that is $4\dfrac{1}{12}$ feet long. Do you have enough wood? Explain.

32. You run the 60-yard dash in $7\dfrac{9}{20}$ seconds. Your friend runs it in $6\dfrac{19}{20}$ seconds. How much faster is your friend's time?

33. Three puppies weigh $1\dfrac{1}{16}$ pounds, $1\dfrac{3}{16}$ pounds, and $\dfrac{15}{16}$ pound. You are carrying all three in a basket. Find the total weight of the three puppies.

LESSON
5.3 **Practice**
For use with pages 230–235

Find the sum or difference.

1. $\dfrac{7}{12} + \dfrac{7}{10}$

2. $\dfrac{8}{9} + \left(-\dfrac{10}{21}\right)$

3. $-\dfrac{4}{17} + \dfrac{3}{5}$

4. $-\dfrac{3}{4} - \left(-\dfrac{5}{18}\right)$

5. $-\dfrac{1}{6} - \dfrac{9}{22}$

6. $-\dfrac{11}{12} - \dfrac{7}{15}$

7. $\dfrac{9}{20} - \dfrac{3}{16}$

8. $-\dfrac{5}{14} - \left(-\dfrac{9}{10}\right)$

Evaluate the expression when $x = \dfrac{5}{6}$ and $y = -\dfrac{3}{10}$.

9. $x + y$

10. $x - y$

11. $y - x$

12. $-y - x$

Find the sum or difference.

13. $5\dfrac{2}{7} + 7\dfrac{1}{6}$

14. $4\dfrac{5}{9} - 3\dfrac{2}{15}$

15. $-2\dfrac{8}{9} + 2\dfrac{5}{6}$

16. $-1\dfrac{5}{8} - \left(-2\dfrac{1}{5}\right)$

17. $1\dfrac{3}{4} - 4\dfrac{3}{14}$

18. $-6\dfrac{3}{25} + 3\dfrac{1}{2}$

19. $4\dfrac{9}{16} + \left(-3\dfrac{3}{10}\right)$

20. $-1\dfrac{2}{3} - \left(-1\dfrac{4}{11}\right)$

Name _____ Date _____

Practice

For use with pages 230–235

Evaluate the expression when $x = -4\frac{1}{6}$ **and** $y = 1\frac{11}{16}$.

21. $x + y$ **22.** $x - y$ **23.** $y - x$ **24.** $-y - x$

Simplify the expression.

25. $-\frac{7x}{6} - \frac{x}{5}$ **26.** $\frac{x}{8} + \frac{5x}{3}$ **27.** $-\frac{2x}{9} + \frac{7x}{15}$ **28.** $\frac{4x}{7} - \frac{8x}{5}$

29. A baby weighs $7\frac{1}{8}$ pounds at birth. After four months, the baby weighs $15\frac{2}{3}$ pounds. How much weight did the baby gain?

30. In a bag of marbles, $\frac{2}{5}$ are red, $\frac{2}{7}$ are green, and the rest are blue. What fraction of the marbles are blue?

31. An ice sculpture originally has a height of $74\frac{1}{4}$ inches. The ice sculpture begins to melt and after several hours, the height has decreased by $8\frac{7}{16}$ inches. What is the current height of the sculpture?

Name _____ Date _____

Practice

For use with pages 237–241

Find the product.

1. $\frac{14}{25} \cdot \left(-\frac{3}{7}\right)$

2. $-\frac{20}{33} \cdot \left(-\frac{3}{11}\right)$

3. $51 \cdot \left(-\frac{5}{6}\right)$

4. $-\frac{7}{22} \cdot (-4)$

5. $2\frac{1}{12} \cdot \left(-10\frac{4}{5}\right)$

6. $-6\frac{3}{16} \cdot 5\frac{3}{7}$

7. $-1\frac{4}{27} \cdot \left(-3\frac{6}{11}\right)$

8. $-5\frac{1}{9} \cdot 2\frac{4}{13}$

Evaluate the expression.

9. $\frac{1}{4} \cdot \frac{8}{9} \cdot \left(-\frac{3}{5}\right)$

10. $\frac{4}{7} \cdot \left(-\frac{1}{8}\right) - \frac{3}{4}$

11. $\frac{7}{10} \cdot \frac{2}{9} + \frac{2}{3}$

Simplify the expression.

12. $\frac{20x}{9} \cdot \frac{36x^4}{5}$

13. $\frac{75x^4}{8} \cdot \frac{14x}{3}$

14. $-\frac{8x}{15} \cdot \left(-\frac{4x}{7}\right)$

15. $-\frac{x^6}{11} \cdot \left(-\frac{5x^8}{3}\right)$

16. $-\frac{13x^2}{10} \cdot \frac{6x^3}{5}$

17. $-\frac{x^6}{12} \cdot \left(-\frac{11x^5}{12}\right)$

18. $\frac{xy}{6} \cdot \frac{2x^3y}{3}$

19. $-\frac{x^2y}{4} \cdot \frac{10y^2}{3}$

Name _____ Date _____

Practice

For use with pages 237–241

Evaluate the expression when $x = -\frac{2}{3}$, $y = \frac{9}{14}$ **and** $z = -\frac{23}{42}$.

20. $x \cdot y + z$ **21.** $y + x \cdot z$ **22.** $x \cdot y \cdot z$ **23.** $z - y \cdot x$

24. A shoreline is eroding at a rate of $2\frac{5}{18}$ feet each year. At this rate, how many feet will the shoreline erode in 8 years?

Find the area of the triangle.

25.

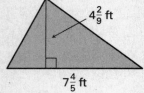

$4\frac{2}{9}$ ft

$7\frac{4}{5}$ ft

26.

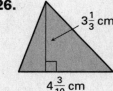

$3\frac{1}{3}$ cm

$4\frac{3}{10}$ cm

27. In a class election, $\frac{5}{6}$ of the students have already voted. Of those students, $\frac{11}{17}$ have voted for Cindy. There are 102 students in the class. How many students voted for Cindy?

LESSON
5.5 Practice

For use with pages 242–246

State the reciprocal of the number.

1. $-\dfrac{24}{7}$

2. -264

3. 3.45

4. 0.01

Find the quotient.

5. $\dfrac{7}{20} \div \dfrac{5}{6}$

6. $-\dfrac{11}{24} \div \dfrac{7}{10}$

7. $\dfrac{8}{33} \div \left(-\dfrac{8}{9}\right)$

8. $-\dfrac{7}{5} \div \dfrac{19}{40}$

9. $8\dfrac{9}{20} \div 1\dfrac{7}{40}$

10. $10\dfrac{9}{14} \div \left(-3\dfrac{1}{2}\right)$

11. $\dfrac{16}{25} \div 2$

12. $48 \div \left(-\dfrac{4}{5}\right)$

13. $12\dfrac{3}{4} \div \left(-\dfrac{11}{12}\right)$

14. $5\dfrac{7}{11} \div 20$

15. $-24\dfrac{4}{9} \div \dfrac{8}{15}$

16. $-\dfrac{10}{33} \div 12$

17. $-\dfrac{18}{35} \div \left(-2\dfrac{4}{5}\right)$

18. $30 \div \left(-4\dfrac{1}{8}\right)$

19. $8\dfrac{7}{10} \div \dfrac{33}{50}$

20. $-\dfrac{15}{26} \div \left(-\dfrac{5}{14}\right)$

Evaluate the expression when $x = -2\dfrac{5}{8}$, $y = \dfrac{3}{10}$, **and** $z = 6\dfrac{3}{4}$.

21. $x \div y$

22. $y \div z$

23. $x \div z$

24. $z \div x \cdot y$

Name _____ Date _____

Practice
For use with pages 242–246

Evaluate the expression.

25. $\dfrac{4}{9} \div \dfrac{1}{3} + \dfrac{7}{10}$

26. $\dfrac{5}{8} + \dfrac{5}{12} \div \dfrac{10}{21}$

27. $-\dfrac{3}{16} \div \left(\dfrac{3}{4} + \dfrac{5}{6}\right)$

28. $\dfrac{23}{41} \div \dfrac{25}{82} - \dfrac{3}{10}$

29. $6\dfrac{7}{8} \div 1\dfrac{5}{6} + \dfrac{11}{20}$

30. $\dfrac{6}{13} \div \dfrac{3}{5} \cdot \dfrac{3}{4}$

31. $-\dfrac{5}{6} \cdot \left(-\dfrac{9}{10}\right) \div \dfrac{17}{20}$

32. $\dfrac{7}{18} \cdot \left(-\dfrac{10}{21}\right) \div \dfrac{11}{9}$

33. $\dfrac{7}{24} \div \left(\dfrac{11}{12} - \dfrac{5}{9}\right)$

34. Evaluate the expression $x^2 \div y$ when $x = -\dfrac{5}{9}$ and $y = -10$.

35. Evaluate the expression $x^2 \div y^2$ when $x = \dfrac{7}{12}$ and $y = -\dfrac{7}{18}$.

36. You have a piece of wood that is $23\dfrac{3}{8}$ feet long. You need to cut pieces that are $1\dfrac{3}{8}$ feet long. How many pieces can you cut?

Name _____ Date _____

Practice

For use with pages 247–252

Solve the equation. Check your solution.

1. $\frac{5}{8}x = 30$

2. $\frac{7}{11}x = 14$

3. $-\frac{7}{12}x = 14$

4. $28 = \frac{14}{15}x$

5. $-\frac{5}{6}x = 20$

6. $-24 = -\frac{12}{19}x$

7. $\frac{7}{11}x = \frac{4}{11}$

8. $\frac{4}{5}x = \frac{7}{5}$

9. $\frac{9}{10}x = \frac{2}{5}$

10. $-\frac{3}{4}x = \frac{11}{32}$

11. $\frac{3}{14} = -\frac{11}{21}x$

12. $-\frac{7}{13}x = \frac{5}{26}$

Solve the equation. Check your solution.

13. $\frac{1}{2}x + 9 = 36$

14. $\frac{4}{7}x + 8 = 28$

15. $6 = \frac{1}{2}x - \frac{1}{4}$

16. $-\frac{2}{3}x + (-10) = 14$

17. $32 = 16 - \frac{1}{2}x$

18. $29 = \frac{9}{11}x + 11$

19. $-\frac{14}{17}x + \frac{13}{17} = \frac{12}{17}$

20. $\frac{5}{11}x + \frac{4}{11} = \frac{3}{11}$

21. $\frac{8}{19} = -\frac{10}{19}x - \frac{9}{19}$

22. $\frac{2}{3}x + \frac{5}{9} = \frac{4}{9}$

23. $\frac{1}{2} = \frac{9}{14}x - \frac{4}{7}$

24. $\frac{8}{21} = -\frac{10}{21}x + \frac{3}{7}$

Name _____ Date _____

Practice

For use with pages 247–252

25. The figure is composed of two rectangles. The area of the figure is
$1\frac{3}{4}$ square inches.

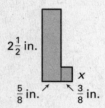

$2\frac{1}{2}$ in.

$\frac{5}{8}$ in. $\frac{3}{8}$ in. x

a. Find the area of the larger rectangle.

b. Write an expression for the area of the smaller rectangle.

c. Write an equation relating the sum of the areas in parts (a) and (b) to the
total area of the figure. Solve the equation to find the value of x.

26. The weight of a bull calf is 388 kilograms. If its weight increases at a rate
of $1\frac{2}{5}$ kilograms per day, how long it will take the bull calf to reach a weight
of 500 kilograms?

LESSON
5.7 **Practice**

For use with pages 253–257

Solve the equation by first clearing the fractions.

1. $-\dfrac{17}{31}x + \dfrac{7}{31} = \dfrac{15}{31}$

2. $\dfrac{1}{12} - \dfrac{2}{3}x = \dfrac{1}{3}$

3. $\dfrac{8}{17}x + \dfrac{5}{34} = \dfrac{6}{17}$

4. $\dfrac{2}{3} = \dfrac{7}{9}x + \dfrac{11}{36}$

5. $\dfrac{1}{6} - \dfrac{1}{3}x = \dfrac{2}{3}$

6. $\dfrac{6}{11} = \dfrac{1}{4} + \dfrac{7}{11}x$

7. $\dfrac{2}{3}x - \dfrac{1}{6} = \dfrac{2}{7}$

8. $\dfrac{7}{20} = \dfrac{1}{6} + \dfrac{1}{2}x$

9. $\dfrac{5}{16} = \dfrac{1}{6} - \dfrac{7}{12}x$

Solve the equation by first clearing the decimals.

10. $2.3x + 9.2 = 23$

11. $9.6 - 2.4x = -24$

12. $-3.9 = 2.6x + 1.56$

13. $6.1x + 20.74 = -51.85$

14. $26.4 = 6.6x + 10.56$

15. $4.5x + 15.3 = -38.25$

16. $1.55 = -3.1x - 0.62$

17. $81.9 = 32.76 + 9.1x$

18. $-0.24 = 0.96 - 0.6x$

Name _____ Date _____

Practice

For use with pages 253–257

Solve the inequality.

19. $\frac{1}{4} \le \frac{1}{16} - \frac{1}{2}x$

20. $-\frac{5}{9}x - \frac{1}{9} < \frac{1}{3}$

21. $\frac{8}{17}x + \frac{5}{34} > \frac{6}{17}$

22. $\frac{9}{40} - \frac{3}{5}x < \frac{1}{2}$

23. $\frac{1}{5} \le \frac{1}{15} - \frac{1}{2}x$

24. $\frac{1}{5} \ge \frac{1}{6} - \frac{2}{3}x$

25. Describe the possible values of x if the area of the rectangle is at least 40 square inches.

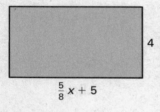

4

$\frac{5}{8}x + 5$

26. You need to exchange some of your U.S. dollars for European euros (€). For every U.S. dollar, you can get €0.866 in European euros. If you already have €187.22 in European euros, how much in U.S. dollars do you need to exchange to have €360.42 in European euros?

LESSON 6.1

Name _____ Date _____

Practice

For use with pages 269–274

Tell whether the ratio is in simplest form. If not, write it in simplest form. Then, write the ratio in two other ways.

1. 4 to 18

2. 4 : 6

3. $\dfrac{7}{9}$

4. $\dfrac{39}{13}$

5. 28 : 21

6. 17 to 44

7. 44 : 16

8. 63 to 18

9. $\dfrac{48}{28}$

Order the ratios from least to greatest.

10. 7 : 2, 12 to 4, $\dfrac{20}{6}$, 21 to 14, 10 : 5

11. $\dfrac{12}{16}$, 7 to 10, 8 : 12, 9 to 15, $\dfrac{4}{18}$

Find the unit rate.

12. $\dfrac{72 \text{ people}}{3 \text{ buses}}$

13. $\dfrac{20 \text{ ounces}}{2.5 \text{ servings}}$

14. $\dfrac{288 \text{ mi}}{12 \text{ gal}}$

15. $\dfrac{10.4 \text{ gal}}{4 \text{ min}}$

16. $\dfrac{1125 \text{ calories}}{4.5 \text{ hours}}$

17. $\dfrac{\$375}{15 \text{ shares}}$

Name _____ Date _____

Practice

For use with pages 269–274

Tell whether the ratios are equivalent.

18. $\dfrac{12}{9}$ and $\dfrac{24}{18}$

19. $14 : 4$ and $21 : 8$

20. 8 to 21 and 48 to 126

Write the equivalent rate.

21. $\dfrac{8 \text{ calls}}{1 \text{ hour}} = \dfrac{? \text{ calls}}{1 \text{ day}}$

22. $\dfrac{1400 \text{ students}}{40 \text{ teachers}} = \dfrac{? \text{ students}}{1 \text{ teacher}}$

23. $\dfrac{12 \text{ km}}{1 \text{ h}} = \dfrac{? \text{ m}}{1 \text{ min}}$

24. Find the ratio of the area of the shaded square region to the area of the unshaded square region.

25. One box of cereal is 20 ounces and costs $3. A smaller box of the same type of cereal is 12 ounces and costs $2. Which box of cereal is the better buy? Explain.

LESSON
6.2 Practice

For use with pages 275–279

Use equivalent ratios to solve the proportion.

1. $\dfrac{2}{7} = \dfrac{24}{x}$

2. $\dfrac{4}{15} = \dfrac{x}{90}$

3. $\dfrac{x}{20} = \dfrac{154}{280}$

4. $\dfrac{x}{13} = \dfrac{70}{91}$

5. $\dfrac{17}{30} = \dfrac{x}{120}$

6. $\dfrac{25}{28} = \dfrac{375}{x}$

7. $\dfrac{x}{35} = \dfrac{96}{210}$

8. $\dfrac{34}{9} = \dfrac{x}{162}$

9. $\dfrac{x}{41} = \dfrac{165}{205}$

Use algebra to solve the proportion.

10. $\dfrac{x}{14} = \dfrac{10}{4}$

11. $\dfrac{x}{22} = \dfrac{20}{5}$

12. $\dfrac{15}{65} = \dfrac{x}{13}$

13. $\dfrac{40}{24} = \dfrac{x}{9}$

14. $\dfrac{63}{93} = \dfrac{x}{31}$

15. $\dfrac{x}{36} = \dfrac{12}{16}$

16. $\dfrac{15}{26} = \dfrac{x}{182}$

17. $\dfrac{x}{108} = \dfrac{15}{12}$

18. $\dfrac{20}{68} = \dfrac{x}{17}$

19. $\dfrac{4.5}{20} = \dfrac{x}{4}$

20. $\dfrac{x}{16.5} = \dfrac{84}{132}$

21. $\dfrac{x}{14} = \dfrac{11}{35}$

Name _____ Date _____

Practice

For use with pages 275–279

In Exercises 22–25, write and solve a proportion to solve the problem.

22. Four notebooks cost $4.40. How many notebooks can you buy for $6.60?

23. Two roses cost $3.50. How many roses can you buy for $17.50?

24. A roll of paper towels cost $1.90. How many rolls can you buy for $9.50?

25. Carl works 8 hours and earns $52. How many hours would he have to work to earn $130?

26. Use the table below that shows the prices of several fruits to answer the following questions.

Fruit	Price
Apples	4 for $3.00
Bananas	3 lb/$1.50
Cantaloupes	2 for $2.50
Cherries	2 lb/$2.40
Peaches	1 lb/$.90

a. How much would 5 pounds of bananas cost?

b. How much would 7 apples cost?

c. You are making a fruit salad for a party. You want to use 5 apples, 2 pounds of bananas, 1 cantaloupe, 1.5 pounds of cherries, and 2 pounds of peaches. How much will the fruit cost for your fruit salad?

Name _____ Date _____

Practice

For use with pages 280–284

Tell whether the ratios form a proportion.

1. $\dfrac{5}{12}, \dfrac{60}{144}$

2. $\dfrac{48}{90}, \dfrac{8}{15}$

3. $\dfrac{52}{16}, \dfrac{39}{10}$

4. $\dfrac{70}{28}, \dfrac{20}{8}$

5. $\dfrac{96}{120}, \dfrac{60}{85}$

6. $\dfrac{9}{6}, \dfrac{156}{104}$

7. $\dfrac{36}{48}, \dfrac{30}{40}$

8. $\dfrac{115}{85}, \dfrac{161}{136}$

Solve the proportion.

9. $\dfrac{14}{24} = \dfrac{21}{x}$

10. $\dfrac{32}{40} = \dfrac{x}{15}$

11. $\dfrac{9}{102} = \dfrac{12}{x}$

12. $\dfrac{28}{x} = \dfrac{8}{16}$

13. $\dfrac{8.4}{x} = \dfrac{8}{20}$

14. $\dfrac{14.6}{23} = \dfrac{x}{11.5}$

15. $\dfrac{18.3}{x} = \dfrac{6.1}{10}$

16. $\dfrac{40}{320} = \dfrac{14}{x}$

17. $\dfrac{12}{x} = \dfrac{0.4}{9}$

18. $\dfrac{3.5}{x} = \dfrac{49}{56}$

19. $\dfrac{0.2}{2.35} = \dfrac{4}{x}$

20. $\dfrac{6.02}{4} = \dfrac{x}{40}$

Practice
For use with pages 280–284

Find the value of x.

21. $\dfrac{30}{48} = \dfrac{15}{x + 9}$

22. $\dfrac{51}{x + 11} = \dfrac{15}{5}$

23. $\dfrac{x - 4}{42} = \dfrac{14}{84}$

24. $\dfrac{35}{20} = \dfrac{13 - x}{28}$

25. $\dfrac{18}{50} = \dfrac{3x}{175}$

26. $\dfrac{22}{38} = \dfrac{33}{2x + 7}$

27. In a batch of 120 manufactured machine parts, 3 are found to be defective. At this rate, how many machine parts would be defective in a batch of 12,000?

28. A post office sells first-class stamps and postcard stamps. For the year, the post office sold 7 first-class stamps for every 2 postcard stamps sold.

   a. The post office sold 46,260 stamps for the year. How many of them were first-class stamps? How many were postcard stamps?

   b. First-class stamps sold for $.37 each. Postcard stamps sold for $.23 each. Write a ratio for the amount of money collected for first-class stamps to the amount of money collected for postcard stamps.

   c. Is the ratio you wrote in part (b) proportional to the ratio of first-class stamps sold to postcard stamps sold?

LESSON
6.4 Practice
For use with pages 287–292

Given *EFGH* ~ *JKLM*, tell whether the statement is *true* or *false*.

1. $\angle F$ and $\angle J$ are corresponding angles.

2. $\overline{GH}$ and $\overline{LM}$ are corresponding sides.

3. $\angle H$ and $\angle M$ are corresponding angles.

4. $\overline{HE}$ and $\overline{MJ}$ are corresponding sides.

5. $\overline{FG}$ and $\overline{KL}$ are corresponding sides.

6. $\angle G$ and $\angle K$ are corresponding angles.

7. Given *DEFG* ~ *RSTU*, name the corresponding angles and the corresponding sides.

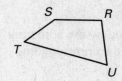

The figures are similar. Find the ratio of the lengths of the corresponding sides of figure A to figure B.

8.

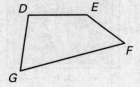

9.

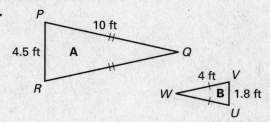
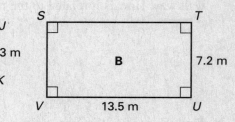

LESSON
6.4
Continued

Name _____ Date _____

Practice

For use with pages 287–292

10.

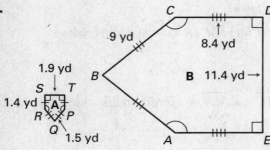

11.

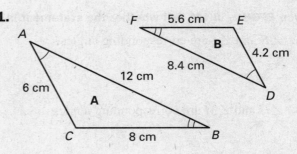

12. A rectangular garden is 49 feet long and 35 feet wide. The garden is bordered by a rectangular walkway that is 56 feet long and 40 feet wide as shown in the figure.

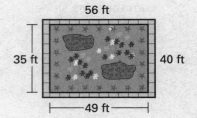

   a. Is the garden area similar to the rectangle formed by the bordering walkway? If so, find the ratio of the lengths of the corresponding sides of the garden to the walkway.

   b. Find the ratio of the perimeter of the garden to the perimeter of the walkway. How is it related to the ratio in part (a)?

   c. Find the ratio of the area of the garden to the area of the garden including the walkway.

Name _____ Date _____

Practice

For use with pages 293–297

Find the specified side length.

1. Given △ABC ~ △JKL, find JK.

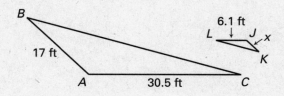

2. Given EFGH ~ STUV, find UV.

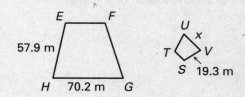

3. Given PQRS ~ WXYZ, find YZ.

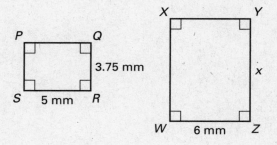

4. Given JKLM ~ PQRS, find QR.

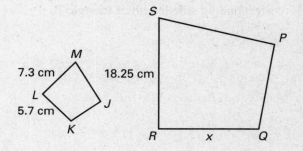

5. Given △PQR ~ △STR, find QT.

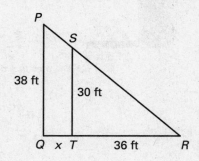

6. Given ABCD ~ AGFE, find GB.

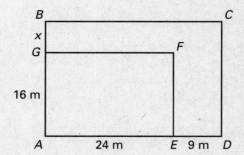

Name _____ Date _____

Practice
For use with pages 293–297

7. The ratio of a side length of rectangle A to a corresponding side length of rectangle B is 12 : 5. Rectangle A has a side length of 60 inches. Find the corresponding side length of rectangle B.

8. The ratio of a side length of triangle A to a corresponding side length of triangle B is 5 : 8. Triangle A has a side length of 18 centimeters. Find the corresponding side length of triangle B.

9. A farmer who is 72 inches tall is standing beside a silo that has a height of 140 feet. The length of the silo's shadow is 31.5 feet. What is the length of the farmer's shadow?

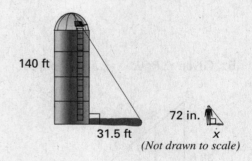

140 ft

31.5 ft

72 in.

x

(Not drawn to scale)

LESSON
6.6

Practice

For use with pages 299–304

A map has a scale of 1 inch : 12 miles. Use the given map distance to find the actual distance.

1. 8 inches

2. 17 inches

3. 25 inches

4. 42 inches

5. $\frac{1}{2}$ inch

6. $\frac{3}{4}$ inch

7. $\frac{3}{8}$ inch

8. $1\frac{1}{8}$ inches

9. $2\frac{1}{2}$ inches

A map has a scale of 1 centimeter : 6 kilometers. Use the given actual distance to find the distance on the map.

10. 24 kilometers

11. 54 kilometers

12. 90 kilometers

13. 33 kilometers

14. 1.8 kilometers

15. 3.6 kilometers

16. 7.2 kilometers

17. 1.5 kilometers

18. 2.7 kilometers

Write the scale without units.

19. 1 in. : 14 ft

20. 1 in. : 30 yd

21. 1 cm : 3 m

22. 1 cm : 65 m

23. 1 cm : 8 km

24. 1 mm : 32 cm

LESSON
6.6
Continued

Name _____ Date _____

Practice

For use with pages 299–304

25. On a map, the distance between two cities is $4\frac{1}{2}$ inches. What is the
actual distance in miles between the two cities if the map's scale is
1 inch : 80 miles?

26. In a scale drawing, a wall is $1\frac{1}{2}$ inches long. The actual wall is 12 feet long.
Find the scale of the drawing.

27. A model of the Transamerica Pyramid in San Francisco, California, has a
scale of 1 : 130. The actual height of the Transamerica Pyramid is 260 meters.
Find the height of the model.

28. A scale model of a football stadium has a scale of 1 : 360.

   a. The actual length of the football field including the end zones is
   120 yards. How long, in inches, is the football field in the model?

   b. How many times the length of the model is the length of the actual
   stadium?

6.7 Practice

For use with pages 305–312

Complete the statement.

1. A(n) _____ probability is based on knowing all of the equally likely outcomes of an experiment.

2. A(n) _____ probability is based on repeated trials of an experiment.

Use the spinner to find the probability. The spinner is divided into equal parts.

3. What is the probability that the spinner stops on a multiple of 3?

4. What is the probability that the spinner stops on a multiple of 4?

5. What are the odds against stopping on a number greater than 8?

6. What are the odds in favor of stopping on a number less than 5?

7. If you spin the spinner 50 times, how many times do you expect it to stop on 10?

Practice

For use with pages 305–312

Each letter in the word SUCCESSES is written on separate slips of paper and placed in a bag. A letter is chosen at random from the bag.

8. What is the probability that the letter chosen is an S?

9. What is the probability that the letter chosen is a vowel?

10. What are the odds against choosing a consonant?

11. A weather forecast says that there is a 40% chance of rain today. Find the odds against rain.

12. You plant 48 seeds of a certain flower and 32 of them sprout. Find the experimental probability that the next flower seed planted will sprout.

The circle graph shows which juice blend people chose as their favorite in a taste test.

13. What is the probability that a person chosen at random chose Juice B?

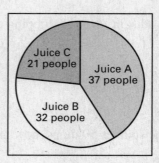

14. What are the odds in favor of choosing a person at random who chose Juice A?

LESSON 6.8 Practice

For use with pages 313–317

In Exercises 1–4, make a tree diagram to find all the possible choices. Check your answer using the counting principle.

1. Choose turkey, roast beef, or ham with white, whole wheat, or rye bread.

2. Choose a sedan, truck, SUV, or minivan in red, blue, black, or green.

3. Choose a T-shirt, a button-down shirt, or a sweater, jeans or khakis, and either a red coat or a blue coat.

4. Choose a ranch, two-story, or tri-level house, white or gray siding, and either a one-car or two-car garage.

5. A menu has 3 choices for salad, 5 main dishes, and 4 desserts. How many different meals are possible if you select a salad, a main dish, and a dessert?

6. You are planning a trip. You can go to Phoenix, Las Vegas, San Diego, or Los Angeles, you can fly or drive, and you can stay for 3, 4, or 5 days. How many possible trips are there?

7. The telephone extensions at a company use 4 digits.

a. How many extensions are possible if there are no restrictions?

b. How many extensions are possible if the first digit cannot be 0 or 9?

c. How many extensions are possible if the first digit can only be 1?

Practice
For use with pages 313–317

8. You are choosing a computer password. The password has 3 letters followed by 3 digits.

    a. How many passwords are possible if the letters must be uppercase?

    b. How many passwords are possible if no letter or digit can be repeated and the letters have to be lowercase?

In Exercises 9 and 10, use the following information. You have a 6-sided number cube and the spinner shown. The spinner is divided into equal parts.

9. You spin the spinner two times. Find the probability that the spinner stops on 3, then 1.

10. You spin the spinner once and roll the number cube once. Find the probability that the spinner stops on the same number that you roll with the number cube.

11. You flip a coin 5 times. What is the probability that the results are all heads or all tails?

12. Each person that works at a company is given a 5-digit code followed by a letter, either uppercase or lowercase. These employees must enter their codes on a keypad to enter and exit the office building. The company has 130 employees.

    a. How many codes are possible if there are no restrictions?

    b. What is the probability of someone entering a code at random and gaining entry to the building?

Name _____ Date _____

Practice

For use with pages 329–333

Write the percent as a fraction.

1. 9%   **2.** 24%   **3.** 53%

4. 91%   **5.** 88%   **6.** 76%

7. 60%   **8.** 44%   **9.** 32%

Write the fraction as a percent.

10. $\frac{49}{50}$ **11.** $\frac{9}{25}$ **12.** $\frac{1}{5}$

13. $\frac{103}{200}$ **14.** $\frac{7}{20}$ **15.** $\frac{93}{100}$

16. $\frac{3}{4}$ **17.** $\frac{11}{50}$ **18.** $\frac{2}{25}$

You spin the spinner shown. Find the probability of the given event. Write your answer as a percent.

19. P(odd)   **20.** P(even)

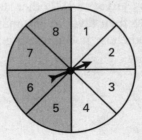

21. P(multiple of 2)   **22.** P(multiple of 3)

23. P(greater than 2)   **24.** P(shaded)

LESSON
7.1
·Continued

Practice

For use with pages 329–333

Find the percent of the number.

25. 60% of 145

26. 90% of 120

27. 32% of 75

28. 56% of 50

29. 64% of 125

30. 12% of 150

31. The circle graph shows the results of a class survey that asked 600 students what their favorite outdoor activity is.

    a. Estimate how many students chose either walking or jogging.

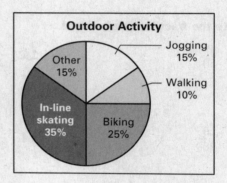

    b. Estimate how many more students chose in-line skating than biking.

    c. The class surveyed 100 other students and found that 23% chose in-line skating as their favorite. Estimate how many students in both surveys combined chose in-line skating as their favorite.

LESSON
7.2 Practice
For use with pages 334–339

Use a proportion to answer the question.

1. What percent of 70 is 21?

2. What percent of 48 is 12?

3. What percent of 56 is 42?

4. What percent of 105 is 63?

5. What number is 42% of 150?

6. What number is 70% of 130?.

7. What number is 48% of 175?

8. What number is 15% of 160?

9. 150 is 15% of what number?

10. 21 is 12% of what number?

11. 198 is 33% of what number?

12. 264 is 55% of what number?

13. The population of a town in 2004 was 12,000. The population of the town in 1994 was 10,800. What percent of the 2004 population is the 1994 population?

14. The Royal Opera House Orchestra in London, England, includes 13 musicians who play the viola. The musicians in the viola section make up $12\frac{1}{2}$% of the orchestra. How many musicians are in the Royal Opera House Orchestra?

Name _____ Date _____

Practice

For use with pages 334–339

15. A bag contains 6 red marbles, 9 blue marbles, and 5 green marbles. You randomly select one marble from the bag. What is the probability that the marble is red? Write your answer as a percent.

16. A greeting card store receives a shipment of cards. The table shows the number of each type of card received.

Type of card	Number of cards
Birthday	72
Good Luck	36
Friendship	92
Get Well	40

   a. What percent of the cards were birthday cards? Good luck cards?

   b. In the shipment, 40% of the cards had yellow envelopes. Of the 72 birthday cards, 18 had yellow envelopes. What percent of the birthday cards had yellow envelopes?

Use a proportion to answer the question in terms of y.

17. What number is 16% of y?

18. What percent of $6y$ is 24?

19. $3y$ is 45% of what number?

20. What percent of $7y$ is 119?

LESSON 7.3

Practice

For use with pages 340–344

Write the decimal as a percent.

1. 0.41

2. 0.93

3. 0.01

4. 3

5. 0.0079

6. 0.061

Write the percent as a decimal.

7. 5%

8. 23%

9. 89%

10. 246%

11. 105.8%

12. 0.073%

13. You are reading a book that has 560 pages. You have read about $\frac{11}{20}$ of the book. What percent of the book have you read?

Write the fraction as a percent.

14. $\frac{19}{30}$

15. $\frac{8}{15}$

16. $\frac{27}{40}$

17. $\frac{15}{9}$

18. $\frac{17}{8}$

19. $\frac{13}{6}$

Practice

For use with pages 340–344

Find the percent of the number.

20. 45% of 18

21. 32% of 110

22. 102% of 150

23. 205% of 40

24. 0.25% of 300

25. 0.361% of 500

26. In 2002, the world population was about 6,234,250,000. In 2002, the population of Europe was about 11.6% of the world's total population. About how many people lived in Europe in 2002?

27. A bag contains a total of 25 marbles. The bag contains white, yellow, and red marbles. You randomly select one marble from the bag. The probability that you select a red marble is 16%. How many red marbles are in the bag?

Use a number line to order the numbers from least to greatest.

28. 248%, 2.56, $\frac{49}{20}$, 2.51, $\frac{127}{50}$

29. 0.0041, $\frac{19}{5000}$, 0.45%, $\frac{7}{2000}$, 0.042

30. 170%, $\frac{41}{25}$, 2, 168%, $\frac{89}{50}$

31. 0.0093, $\frac{6}{625}$, 0.094, 0.91%, $\frac{19}{2000}$

Evaluate the expression when $m = 25$.

32. m% of 70

33. 3% of m

34. 130% of m

LESSON
7.4 Practice
For use with pages 345–349

1. Describe and correct the error in using the percent equation to find what percent of 125 is 82.

$$a = p\% \cdot b$$
$$82 = p\% \cdot 125$$
$$\frac{82}{125} = p\%$$
$$0.656\% = p\%$$

Use the percent equation to answer the question.

2. What number is 92% of 115?

3. What number is 35% of 80?

4. What number is 21% of 60?

5. What number is 6% of 25?

6. What percent of 70 is 42?

7. What percent of 325 is 78?

8. What percent of 152 is 95?

9. What percent of 315 is 126?

10. 88 is 32% of what number?

11. 49 is 35% of what number?

12. 124 is 80% of what number?

13. 82 is 4% of what number?

14. A car salesperson earns 1.5% commission on every car sold. The salesperson sells a car for $22,500. What is the commission?

15. At the concession stand of a school football game, sandwiches cost $1.50 and a bottle of water costs $.90. The school sells 40 sandwiches and 80 bottles of water.

   a. How much money was made from selling sandwiches? Bottles of water?

   b. What percent of the money came from sales of sandwiches?

   c. What percent of the concessions sold was bottles of water?

16. Due to a membership drive for a public television station, the current membership is 125% of what it was a year ago. The current membership is 1200. How many members did the station have last year?

17. Randal answers 96 out of 120 questions correctly on a science exam. What percent of the questions did Randal answer correctly?

Use the percent equation to answer the question when $n = 55$.

18. What is $(n - 5)\%$ of 150?

19. What percent of 900 is $(n + 20)$?

20. $(3n)$ is 20% of what number?

21. What is $(2n)\%$ of 540?

LESSON
7.5 **Practice**
For use with pages 351–356

Find the percent of increase or decrease.

1. Original: 400
New: 552

2. Original: 800
New: 1216

3. Original: 1100
New: 1969

4. Original: 1700
New: 3094

5. Original: 475
New: 589

6. Original: 175
New: 259

7. Original: 600
New: 174

8. Original: 240
New: 156

9. Original: 4500
New: 4005

10. Original: 900
New: 324

11. Original: 650
New: 91

12. Original: 1460
New: 657

Find the new amount.

13. Increase 300 by 54%.

14. Increase 2850 by 18%.

15. Increase 1425 by 4%.

16. Decrease 280 by 95%.

17. Decrease 225 by 68%.

18. Decrease 700 by 49%.

Name _____ Date _____

Practice
For use with pages 351–356

19. Last year, 12,500 people participated in a charity 10K walk. This year, 14,000 people participated in the walk. By what percent did the number of participants change from last year to this year?

20. In 1991, sporting good stores sold about $15 billion in merchandise. In 2001, sporting good stores sold about $28 billion in merchandise. Find the percent of change from 1991 to 2001.

21. An antique ceramic pitcher is being sold at an online auction. The minimum bid is $125. At the end of the auction, the pitcher is sold for 288% above the minimum bid. What is the selling price of the pitcher?

22. The bar graph shows the number of entrants in an annual cooking contest from 1997 through 2003.

    a. Find the percent of change from 1997 to 1999.

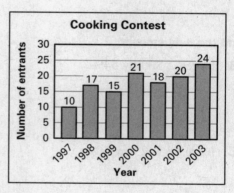

    b. Find the percent of change from 1999 to 2003.

    c. Find the percent of change from 1997 to 2003.

Name _____ Date _____

Practice

For use with pages 357–361

n Exercises 1–6, use the given information to find the new price.

1. Wholesale price: $5
Markup percent: 125%

2. Wholesale price: $92
Markup percent: 45%

3. Wholesale price: $210
Markup percent: 30%

4. Original price: $33
Discount percent: 20%

5. Original price: $76
Discount percent: 35%

6. Original price: $106
Discount percent: 70%

7. A video game is on sale for 15% off the retail price of $45. A store is
having a sale on all video games, providing an additional 20% off of all
sale prices. What is the new sale price of the video game?

In Exercises 8–15, use the given information to find the total cost.

8. Original price: $16
Sales tax: 6%

9. Original price: $28
Sales tax: 4.5%

10. Original price: $49
Sales tax: 7%

11. Original price: $82
Sales tax: 5.5%

12. Food bill: $55
Sales tax: 8%
Tip: 18%

13. Food bill: $68
Sales tax: 3%
Tip: 20%

Name _____ Date _____

Practice

For use with pages 357–361

14. Food bill: $80.40
Sales tax: 5%
Tip: 10%

15. Food bill: $30
Sales tax: 5.5%
Tip: 15%

16. A shoe store is having a sale on sneakers. You want to buy a pair of sneakers that originally cost $75. The sales tax is 4% and it will be applied to the sale price of the sneakers. What is the total cost of the sneakers?

17. The food bill for your breakfast is $16.85. You leave a 10% tip. The sales tax is 5%. What is the total cost, to the nearest cent, of your meal?

In Exercises 18–21, use the given information to find the original price.

18. Retail price: $99
Markup percent: 80%

19. Retail price: $67.60
Markup percent: 150%

20. Sale price: $32.45
Discount percent: 45%

21. Sale price: $48.79
Discount percent: 15%

Name _____ Date _____

Practice

For use with pages 362–367

For an account that earns simple annual interest, find the interest and the balance of the account. Round your answer to the nearest cent, if necessary.

1. $P = \$100$, $r = 3.5\%$, $t = 5$ years

2. $P = \$525$, $r = 6\%$, $t = 9$ years

3. $P = \$400$, $r = 4\%$, $t = 12$ years

4. $P = \$1100$, $r = 2\%$, $t = 15$ years

5. $P = \$900$, $r = 5\%$, $t = 45$ months

6. $P = \$1050$, $r = 3.1\%$, $t = 27$ months

Find the unknown quantity for an account that earns simple annual interest.

7. $A = \$875$, $P = \$500$,
   $r = $ __?__ , $t = 30$ years

8. $A = \$1128.50$, $P = \$925$,
   $r = 5.5\%$, $t = $ __?__

9. $A = \$1213.60$, $P = \$800$,
   $r = 4.7\%$, $t = $ __?__

10. $A = \$2719.50$, $P = $ __?__ ,
   $r = 6.1\%$, $t = 20$ years

11. A \$700 bond earns 3.5% simple annual interest. What is the interest earned after 21 years?

12. Kendall loans Reagan \$500 and charges her 2% simple annual interest. Reagan promises to repay Kendall in 14 months. About how much will Reagan have to pay Kendall? Round your answer to the nearest cent.

Name _____ Date _____

Practice

For use with pages 362–367

13. The table shows three accounts that earn simple annual interest. Complete the table by finding the unknown quantity.

Balance	Principal	Interest rate	Time
$1286.25		7.5%	3 years
$2610.85	$2020	9%	
$3742.50	$3000		45 months

14. You deposit $250 into an account that earns 7.2% simple annual interest. After how many years will the account have a balance of $700?

For an account that earns interest compounded annually, use a calculator to find the balance of the account. Round your answer to the nearest cent.

15. $P = \$900$, $r = 5\%$, $t = 3$ years

16. $P = \$4000$, $r = 8.2\%$, $t = 10$ years

17. $P = \$600$, $r = 9.3\%$, $t = 2$ years

18. $P = \$2000$, $r = 7.5\%$, $t = 20$ years

19. You deposit $575 into a savings account that earns 4.6% interest compounded annually. Use a calculator to find the new balance of the account after 4 years. Round your answer to the nearest cent.

20. The accounts shown earn interest compounded annually. Which account will have the greater balance in the given time?

Account A	Account B
Principal: $405	Principal: $405
Interest rate: 7.2%	Interest rate: 5.3%
Time: 15 years	Time: 30 years

LESSON 8.1 Practice

For use with pages 385–390

Identify the domain and range of the relation.

1. $(5, 0), (6, 0), (7, 6), (8, 8), (8, 10)$

2. $(-6, 4), (-3, 0), (4, 2), (4, 3), (7, 9)$

3.

x	−4	−4	−1	3	4
y	−5	−4	−3	2	0

4.

x	0	0	2	4	8
y	−3	−1	1	3	−1

Represent the relation as a graph and as a mapping diagram. Then tell whether the relation is a function. Explain your reasoning.

5. $(-2, 2), (-1, 2), (1, 2), (2, 2)$

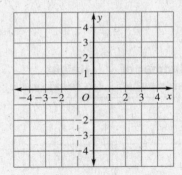

6. $(0, 0), (1, 1), (1, 2), (3, 3), (4, 4)$

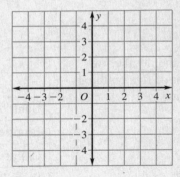

7.

x	−2	−1	0	1	2
y	1	2	2	1	0

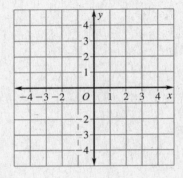

8.

x	2	4	1	2	5
y	3	1	3	2	4

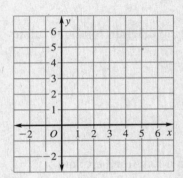

Name _____ Date _____

Practice

For use with pages 385–390

In Exercises 9–11, tell whether the relation represented by the graph is a function.

9.
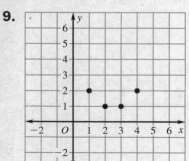

10.
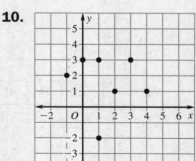

11.
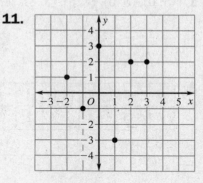

12. Twenty children line up to ride go-carts. The go-cart operator collects $2 from each child in order from the 1st to the 20th in the line. Do the ordered pairs (child number, amount paid) represent a function? Explain your reasoning.

13. The table shows the number of stories and height of five buildings in the United States.

Building	Number of stories, x	Height (in feet), y
Bank of America Plaza	55	1023
Empire State Building	102	1250
Library Tower	75	1018
Sears Tower	110	1450
JP Morgan Chase Tower	75	1002

a. Identify the domain and range of the relation given by the ordered pairs (x, y).

b. Draw a mapping diagram for the relation.

c. Is the relation a function? Explain.

LESSON
8.2 **Practice**

For use with pages 391–397

Tell whether the ordered pair is a solution of the equation.

1. $y = 5x$; $(15, -3)$

2. $y = 4x + 9$; $(-2, 1)$

3. $4x - 5y = 1$; $(4, 3)$

4. $7y - 3x = 11$; $(5, 8)$

Find the value of d when r has the given value in the equation.

5. $d = 2.5r$; $r = 64$

6. $d = 3r + 120$; $r = 62$

7. $d - 5r = 40$; $r = 4$

8. $12r - d = -240$; $r = 9$

Graph the equation. Tell whether the equation is a function.

9. $y = x - 3$

10. $y = 2x + 4$

11. $y = -\dfrac{3}{4}x$

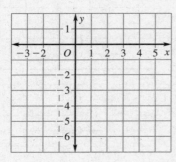

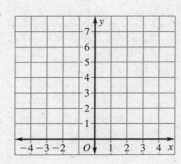

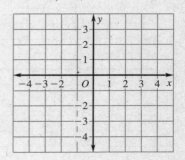

12. $y = -\dfrac{1}{3}x + 2$

13. $x = -11$

14. $y = 8$

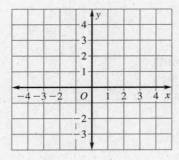

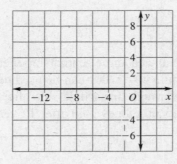

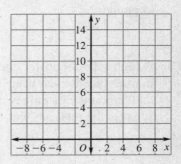

15. $x = 8$

16. $y = -1$

17. $y = 2(x + 1)$

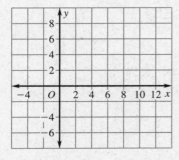

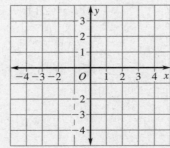

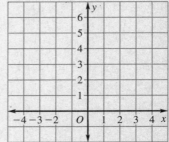

Name _____   Date _____

Practice

For use with pages 391–397

Write the equation in function form. Then graph the equation.

18. $7x - y = 0$

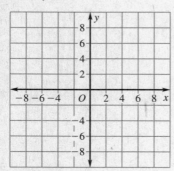

19. $15x + y = 20$

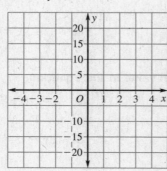

20. $y + 6x - 12 = 0$

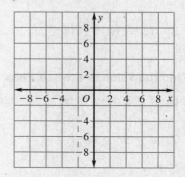

21. $6y - 3x = 12$

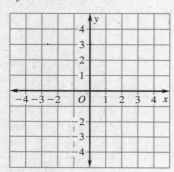

22. $3x - 2y = 6$

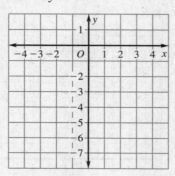

23. $4x - 12y + 24 = 0$

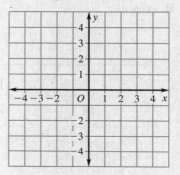

24. The formula $y = 2.205x$ converts a mass x in kilograms to a weight y in pounds. A sports car has a mass of 1270 kilograms. What is its weight in pounds?

25. A high school booster club sets up an academic scholarship that is awarded to one student each year. The formula $y = 2700x$ can be used to find the total amount y of money awarded through this scholarship after x years. What is the total amount of scholarship money paid after 12 years?

Find the value of a that makes the ordered pair a solution of the equation.

26. $y = 3x + 7; (-3, a)$

27. $y = 11 - 7x; (a, -10)$

28. $2x + 4y = 14; (-5, a)$

29. $9x - 5y = -9; (a - 1, 9)$

Name _____ Date _____

Practice

For use with pages 398–402

Identify the *x*-intercept and the *y*-intercept of the line.

1.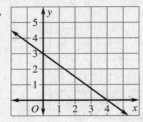

2.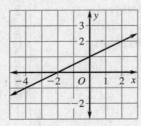

3.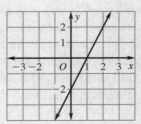

Find the intercepts of the equation's graph. Then graph the equation.

4. $-x + 3y = -9$

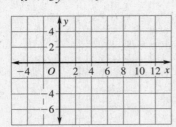

5. $2x + 5y = -20$

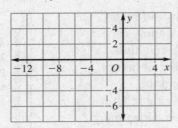

6. $-3x + 4y = 36$

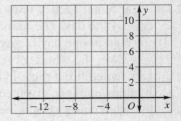

7. $6x + 7y = 42$

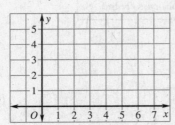

8. $4x + 5y = -60$

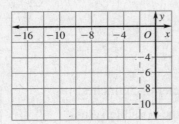

9. $2x + y = 14$

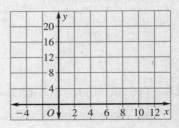

10. $-\dfrac{1}{3}x + \dfrac{7}{6}y = -\dfrac{7}{3}$

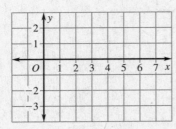

11. $-\dfrac{3}{5}x + \dfrac{1}{5}y = \dfrac{9}{5}$

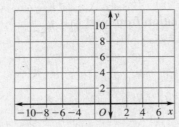

12. $\dfrac{3}{8}x + \dfrac{1}{2}y = -3$

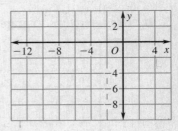

13. $-21.9x + 6.57y = 65.7$

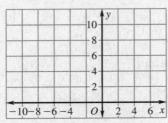

14. $-8.5x + 13.6y = -68$

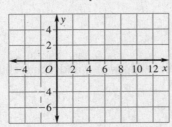

15. $-6.5x + 1.3y = 3.25$

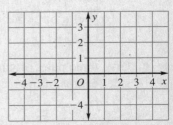

Name _____ Date _____

Practice

For use with pages 398–402

16. You are in charge of buying salads for a picnic. You have $20 and plan to buy potato salad and pasta salad. Potato salad costs $1.25 per pound, and pasta salad costs $2.50 per pound. Write an equation describing the possible amounts of potato salad and pasta salad that you can buy. Use intercepts to graph the equation.

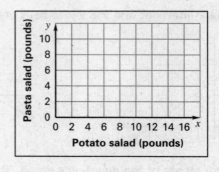

17. A car rental agency rents economy and luxury cars by the day. The number of economy cars y rented in one day is given by the equation $y = 24 - 4x$, where x is the number of luxury cars rented. Find the x-intercept and the y-intercept of the given equation's graph. Use the intercepts to graph the equation. How many economy cars are rented when 4 luxury cars have been rented?

18. The rectangle shown has a perimeter of 52 inches.

   a. Write an equation describing the possible values of x and y.

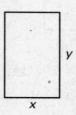

   b. Use intercepts to graph the equation from part (a).

   c. Give three pairs of whole-number values of x and y that could represent side lengths of the rectangle.

LESSON
8.4 Practice

Name _____ Date _____

For use with pages 403–409

Tell whether the slope of the line is *positive*, *negative*, *zero*, or *undefined*. Then find the slope.

1.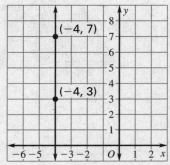

2.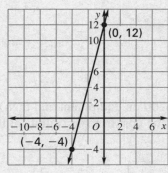

3.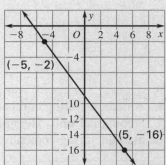

Find the coordinates of two points on the line with the given equation. Then use the points to find the slope of the line.

4. $y = -3x + 11$

5. $y = -17$

6. $y = \frac{7}{8}x - 11$

7. $9x + 8y = 56$

8. $x = 10$

9. $7y - 3x = -147$

Find the slope of the line through the given points.

10. $(6, 3), (14, 19)$

11. $(10, 11), (15, 16)$

12. $(8, 48), (16, 24)$

13. $(1, 5), (36, 19)$

14. $(4, 4), (32, 18)$

15. $(9, 4), (32, 17)$

16. $(-6, -17), (-22, -12)$

17. $(-9, -7), (-11, -13)$

18. $(7, -20), (-13, 10)$

19. $(2, -11), (-13, 14)$

20. $(-4, 15), (-9, 11)$

21. $(4, 4), (14, 10)$

LESSON
8.4
Continued
Practice
For use with pages 403–409

Name _____ Date _____

22. The slope of the roof of a house is called the pitch of the roof. Find the pitch of the roof shown.

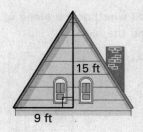

15 ft

9 ft

23. A manufacturing company spent $700 on equipment and then a fixed amount per unit. The graph shows the cost to make x units at the manufacturing company.

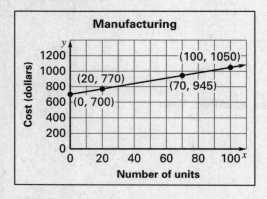

Manufacturing

Cost (dollars)

(100, 1050)
(20, 770)
(70, 945)
(0, 700)

Number of units

a. Find the slope of the line.

b. What information about the company can you obtain from the slope?

c. A second manufacturing company spent $700 on equipment and $2.50 per unit. Suppose you made a graph showing the cost to make x units at the second manufacturing company. How would the graph of the second company compare with the graph of the first company? Explain your thinking.

LESSON
8.6 Practice

For use with pages 419–425

Write an equation of the line with the given slope and *y*-intercept.

1. slope $= -3$; *y*-intercept $= -2$

2. slope $= 5$; *y*-intercept $= 7$

3. slope $= -\dfrac{3}{4}$; *y*-intercept $= 3$

4. slope $= \dfrac{5}{2}$; *y*-intercept $= -6$

Write an equation of the line.

5.
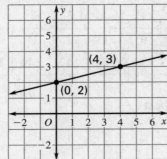

6.
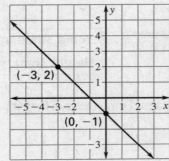

7.
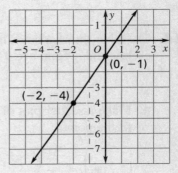

In Exercises 8–10, write an equation of the line through the given points.

8. $(0, 4)$, $(3, 3)$

9. $(2, -3)$, $(0, 5)$

10. $(0, -2)$, $(3, -2)$

In Exercises 11 and 12, use the graph at the right.

11. Write an equation of the line that is parallel to line *a* and passes through the point $(0, 9)$.

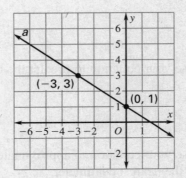

12. Write an equation of the line perpendicular to line *a* that passes through the point $(0, -2)$.

Practice

For use with pages 419–425

13. Show that the table represents a function. Then write an equation for the function.

x	−4	−2	0	2	4
y	5	4	3	2	1

14. The table shows a boy's height measured each birthday from age 9 until age 13.

Years since age 9, x	0	1	2	3	4
Height (cm), y	133	139	143	149	156

    a. Make a scatter plot of the data pairs. Draw the line that appears to best fit the points.

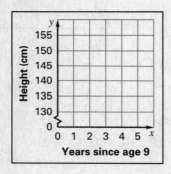

    b. Write an equation of your line.

    c. Use your equation to predict the boy's height at age 17.

    d. Use your equation to approximate the boy's height on his 8th birthday to the nearest centimeter.

LESSON
8.7 **Practice**
For use with pages 426–430

Let $f(x) = 4x - 3$ and $h(x) = -5x + 7$. Find the indicated value.

1. $f(x)$ when $x = 6$

2. $h(x)$ when $x = -5$

3. x when $f(x) = -15$

4. x when $h(x) = -13$

5. $f(-3) + h(2)$

6. $f(5) - h(0)$

Graph the function.

7. $g(x) = 9x - 7$

8. $h(x) = -\frac{4}{5}x + 1$

9. $f(x) = \frac{2}{7}x - 3$

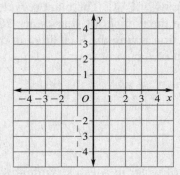

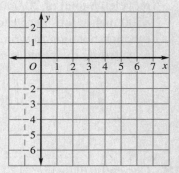

Write a linear function that represents the graph.

10.

11.

12.

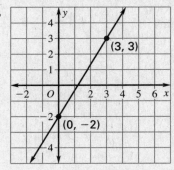

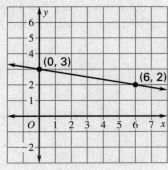

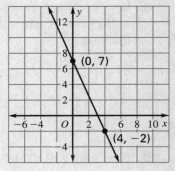

Name _____ Date _____

Practice

For use with pages 426–430

Write a linear function that satisfies the given conditions.

13. $f(0) = 40, f(30) = 65$ **14.** $f(-7) = 8, f(0) = 12$

15. $d(-13) = -9, d(0) = -2$ **16.** $g(0) = 111, g(25) = 286$

17. A PVC (polyvinylchloride) recycling plant uses recent technology to separate PVC from scrap by dissolving the PVC. By 2004, the plant had recycled a total of 20,000 metric tons of PVC. The plant recycles about 8500 metric tons per year. Let t be the number of years since 2004. Use function notation to write an equation giving the total amount of PVC recycled by the plant as a function of t.

18. Currently, there are 4120 gallons of water in Alexa's swimming pool. When filled to the recommended level, the pool holds 4550 gallons. Using a garden hose, she adds 6 gallons of water per minute to the pool.

a. Use function notation to write an equation giving the amount of water in the pool as a function of the number of minutes x that Alexa runs the hose.

b. How long will it take Alexa to fill the pool?

Name _____ Date _____

Practice

For use with pages 431–435

Tell whether the ordered pair is a solution of the linear system.

1. $(-2, 1)$

$y - 2x = 5$

$2y + 2x = -2$

2. $(2, 4)$

$2y - x = 3$

$y + 4 = 4x$

3. $(3, -2)$

$2y - \frac{2}{3}x = 6$

$\frac{1}{2}y + 2x = 5$

In Exercises 4–12, solve the linear system by graphing.

4. $y = 4$

$x = 3$

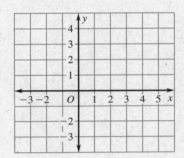

5. $y = -3x - 7$

$15x + 5y = -35$

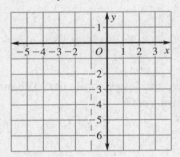

6. $y = 3x + 3$

$y + 3x = 3$

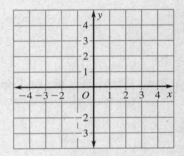

7. $4x + 5y = 10$

$3x - 3y = 21$

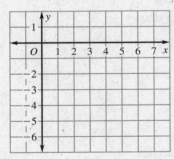

8. $6x - 10y = -10$

$5y = 3x + 5$

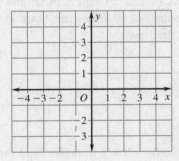

9. $6x - 4y = -2$

$-3x + 5y = -11$

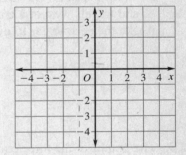

10. $y = \frac{3}{4}x + 8$

$4y = 3x + 4$

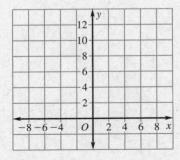

11. $\frac{3}{2}y - x = 3$

$3y = 2x - 6$

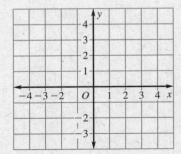

12. $\frac{4}{5}x - \frac{2}{5}y = 2$

$2y = -3x + 4$

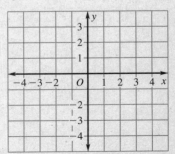

Name _____ Date _____

Practice

For use with pages 431–435

13. You are planning a family reunion. You have two options to pay for food and the banquet hall. For the first option, you can pay $240 for the use of the banquet hall and pay a caterer $8 per person for food. For the second option, the banquet hall will also furnish the food for $600.

 a. Write a system of equations describing the total cost of the family reunion.

 b. Solve the system of equations. After how many family members are the two options equal?

 c. When does the first option have the lower total cost? When does the second option have the lower cost?

14. A car enters a highway at point *A* and travels west at a constant speed of 55 miles per hour. One hour later, another car enters the highway at point *A*, and travels west at a constant speed of 65 miles per hour. How long does it take the second car to overtake the first?

15. The graphs of the three equations below form a triangle. Find the coordinates of the triangle's vertices.

 $4x + y = 1$

 $2x - y = 5$

 $3y + 3x = 12$

Practice

For use with pages 436–441

Describe and correct the error in the graph of the given inequality.

1. $y \leq -\dfrac{5}{6}x + 3$

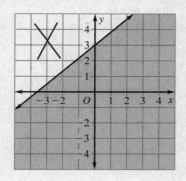

2. $y > -4x$

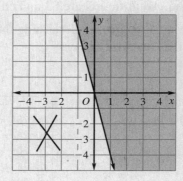

Tell whether the ordered pair is a solution of the inequality.

3. $y \leq -9x - 1; (-1, -5)$

4. $y < 2x + 3; (2, 2)$

5. $x \geq -7; (3, -1)$

6. $2x + 3y > 15; (1, 4)$

Graph the inequality in a coordinate plane.

7. $-3x - 4y > -36$

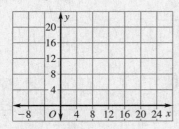

8. $7x + 4y < -32$

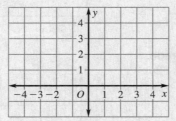

9. $10y - 3x \leq -50$

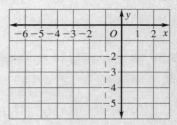

10. $2x + y \geq 21$

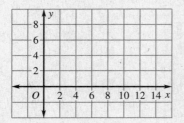

11. $9y - 4x \geq 18$

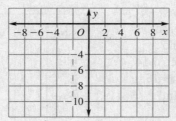

12. $x + 2y < -11$

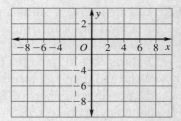

13. $y > -1$

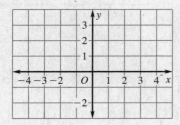

14. $x \geq 5$

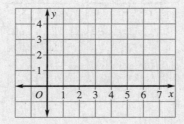

15. $y \leq 3$

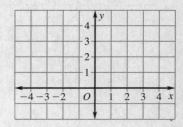

Name _____ Date _____

Practice

For use with pages 436–441

16. You have $42 to spend on museum tickets for a group of adults and children. Adult tickets are $3 and child tickets are $1.50.

   a. Write an inequality describing the possible numbers of adult and child tickets that you can buy.

   b. Graph the inequality from part (a).

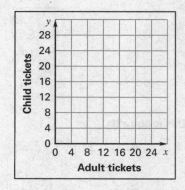

   c. Give three possible combinations of adult and child tickets that you can buy.

17. You are selling T-shirts and buttons as a fund-raiser for your soccer team. You want to earn at least $136. The T-shirts cost $12 and the buttons cost $4. Write and graph an inequality describing the possible numbers of T-shirts and buttons you could sell.

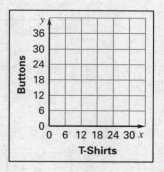

Write an inequality to represent the graph.

18.

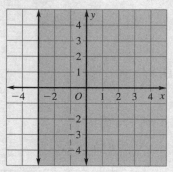

19.

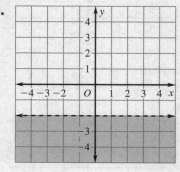

20.

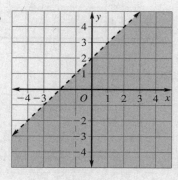

LESSON 9.1

Practice

For use with pages 453–457

Name _____ **Date** _____

Find the square roots of the number.

1. 36

2. 361

3. 729

4. 1089

5. 4900

6. 10,000

Approximate the square root to the nearest integer.

7. $\sqrt{39}$

8. $-\sqrt{85}$

9. $\sqrt{105}$

10. $-\sqrt{136}$

11. $\sqrt{17.4}$

12. $-\sqrt{3.3}$

Use a calculator to approximate the square root. Round to the nearest tenth.

13. $\sqrt{5}$

14. $-\sqrt{12}$

15. $\sqrt{102}$

16. $-\sqrt{74}$

17. $\sqrt{1585}$

18. $\sqrt{27.8}$

Evaluate the expression when $a = 72$ and $b = 8$.

19. $\sqrt{a-b}$

20. $\sqrt{a+b+1}$

21. $-4\sqrt{ab}$

Name _____ Date _____

Practice
For use with pages 453–457

Solve the equation. Round to the nearest tenth if necessary.

22. $x^2 = 64$

23. $y^2 = 324$

24. $225 = n^2$

25. $t^2 = 42$

26. $150 = c^2$

27. $5y^2 = 48$

Solve the equation. Round to the nearest hundredth if necessary.

28. $2x^2 = 32$

29. $90 = 1.5t^2 + 8$

30. $5n^2 - 4 = 74$

31. A square ice skating rink has an area of 1849 square feet. What is the perimeter of the rink?

32. A forest ranger is stationed in a 58 foot tall fire tower. The equation for the distance in miles that the ranger can see is $d = \sqrt{1.5h}$, where h is the height in feet above the ground. Find the distance the ranger can see. Round your answer to the nearest tenth.

LESSON
9.2

Practice

For use with pages 458–461

Simplify the expression.

1. $\sqrt{54}$

2. $\sqrt{112}$

3. $\sqrt{176}$

4. $\sqrt{180}$

5. $\sqrt{117f}$

6. $\sqrt{432y^2}$

7. $\sqrt{\dfrac{120}{121}}$

8. $\sqrt{\dfrac{75}{225}}$

9. $\sqrt{\dfrac{202}{256}}$

10. $\sqrt{\dfrac{320}{441}}$

11. $\sqrt{\dfrac{21v^2}{324}}$

12. $\sqrt{\dfrac{94t}{196}}$

13. A square has an area of 700 square units. Find the length of a side of the square as a radical expression in simplest form.

Simplify the expression.

14. $\sqrt{171cd^2}$

15. $\sqrt{152m^2n}$

16. $\sqrt{126x^2y^2}$

17. $\sqrt{\dfrac{23w^2}{49}}$

18. $\sqrt{\dfrac{45rt^2}{144}}$

19. $\sqrt{\dfrac{76p^2q^2}{81}}$

Name _____ Date _____

Practice

For use with pages 458–461

20. After a car accident on a dry asphalt road, an investigator measures the length ℓ (in feet) of a car's skid marks. The expression $\sqrt{18\ell}$ gives the car's speed in miles per hour at the time the brakes were applied.

   a. Write the expression in simplest form.

   b. The skid marks are 140 feet long. Use the simplified expression to approximate the car's speed when the brakes were applied.

21. You drop a stick from the top of a building that is 245 feet high. You can use the expression $\sqrt{\dfrac{245}{16}}$ to find the time in seconds that it takes the stick to hit the ground. Write the expression in simplest form. Then approximate the value of the expression to the nearest second.

LESSON 9.3 **Practice**

For use with pages 464–469

Find the unknown length. Write your answer in simplest form.

1.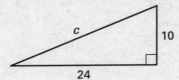

2.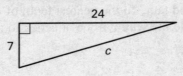

3.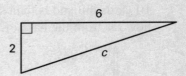

4.

5.

6.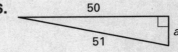

Determine whether the triangle with the given side lengths is a right triangle.

7. 8, 15, 17

8. 20, 21, 28

9. 9, 12, 15

10. 11, 13, 17

11. 5, 64, 65

12. 12, 25, 27

The lengths of two sides of a right triangle are given. Find the length of the third side.

13. $a = 9, c = 41$

14. $a = 40, c = 58$

15. $b = 56, c = 65$

16. $b = 70, c = 74$

17. $a = 13, b = 84$

18. $a = 16, b = 63$

Name _____ Date _____

Practice

For use with pages 464–469

19. A support wire 12 yards long is attached to the top of a utility pole
10 yards tall and is then stretched taut. To the nearest tenth of a yard, find
how far from the base of the pole the wire will be attached to the ground.

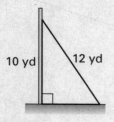

10 yd   12 yd

20. An access ramp has a height of 5 feet and a horizontal distance of 60 feet.
Find the length ℓ of the ramp to the nearest tenth of a foot.

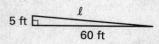

5 ft ℓ

60 ft

Find the unknown length. Round to the nearest hundredth, if necessary.

21.

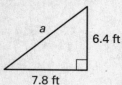

a 6.4 ft

7.8 ft

22.   10.6 cm

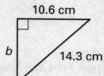

b 14.3 cm

23.

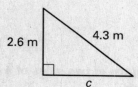

2.6 m   4.3 m

c

Name _____ Date _____

Practice

For use with pages 470–474

Tell whether the number is *rational* or *irrational*.

1. $\frac{1}{7}$

2. $\sqrt{\frac{1}{7}}$

3. $1.\overline{12}$

4. $-\sqrt{17}$

5. $-\sqrt{\frac{8}{2}}$

6. $\sqrt{\frac{21}{3}}$

7. $\frac{\sqrt{5}}{16}$

8. $\frac{\sqrt{16}}{5}$

Complete the statement using <, >, or =.

9. $\sqrt{\frac{1}{4}}$ ____ $\frac{1}{4}$

10. 4 ____ $\sqrt{\frac{32}{2}}$

11. $-\sqrt{8}$ ____ $-\frac{10}{3}$

In Exercises 12–15, use a number line to order the numbers from least to greatest.

12. $\frac{12}{11}, \sqrt{1.1}, \frac{\sqrt{10}}{3}, \sqrt{\frac{10}{3}}$

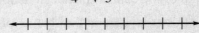

13. $4.2, \sqrt{17}, \frac{17}{4}, \sqrt{\frac{81}{5}}$

14. $\sqrt{\frac{5}{9}}, \frac{2}{3}, \sqrt{\frac{7}{9}}, 0.7514, 0.\overline{75}$

15. $\sqrt{31}, 5.5, \frac{\sqrt{75}}{2}, \frac{28}{5}, \sqrt{\frac{55}{2}}$

Name _____   Date _____

Practice

For use with pages 470–474

16. One leg of a right triangle is 6 inches long. The other leg is 8 inches long. Is the length in inches of the hypotenuse a *rational* or *irrational* number?

17. From a balcony, you drop a penny 50 feet to the ground. The time t in seconds it takes the penny to hit the ground is approximated by $t = \sqrt{\dfrac{25}{8}}$. Does t represent a rational or an irrational number of seconds? Give the value of t to the nearest hundredth of a second.

18. You want to buy some frozen pizzas that have a diameter of 18 inches. You need to be able to fit them into your upright freezer that has a capacity of 4.5 cubic feet. The storage compartment of the freezer is 2 feet high. The width and depth of the compartment can be found using the expression $\sqrt{\dfrac{4.5}{2}}$. Will the pizzas lay flat on the shelves of your freezer? Explain.

19. Use a right triangle to graph $\sqrt{8}$ on a number line.

Name _____   Date _____

Practice

For use with pages 476–481

Find the distance between the points. Write your answer in simplest form.

1. A and B

2. B and C

3. C and D

4. D and A

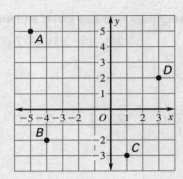

Find the distance between the points. Write your answer in simplest form.

5. $(-12, -8)$, $(3, 11)$ **6.** $(0, 7)$, $(-2, -1)$ **7.** $(1.5, -2)$, $(-4, 6)$

8. $(4.9, -1)$, $(7.4, -6)$ **9.** $(5.5, -3)$, $(2.5, -7)$ **10.** $(4, -3.5)$, $(-2, 8.5)$

Find the midpoint of the segment.

11. $\overline{GH}$ **12.** $\overline{HE}$

13. $\overline{EF}$ **14.** $\overline{FG}$

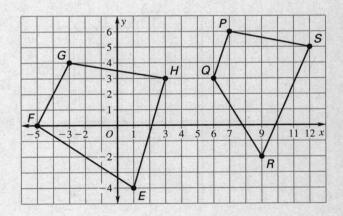

Find the slope of the line through the given points.

15. P and Q **16.** Q and R

17. R and S **18.** P and S

Practice

For use with pages 476–481

Find the midpoint of the segment with the given endpoints.

19. $(-9, -8), (1, 2)$

20. $(4, -5), (-2, 7)$

21. $(1.6, 0), (5.4, -3)$

22. $(-3.2, -1.2), (7.8, 6.8)$

23. $(-12, 5.4), (14, 3.6)$

24. $\left(15, -3\frac{1}{2}\right), (13, -1)$

Find the slope of the line through the given points.

25. $(8, -12), (10, -3)$

26. $(-9, 11), (7, -5)$

27. $(3.2, 7), (1.6, -9)$

28. $(6, -4.5), (1, -3.7)$

29. $\left(4\frac{3}{4}, -6\right), \left(1\frac{1}{4}, 5\right)$

30. $\left(12, \frac{9}{10}\right), \left(-11, \frac{3}{10}\right)$

31. The points $P(-4, 6)$, $Q(-4, -3)$, and $R(8, -3)$ are the vertices of a right triangle in a coordinate plane.

    a. Draw the triangle in a coordinate plane.

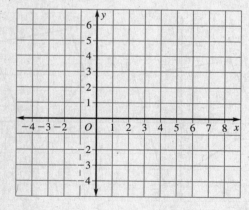

    b. Find the coordinates of the midpoint M of the hypotenuse of $\triangle PQR$.

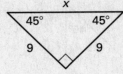

Practice

For use with pages 482–487

Find the unknown length. Write your answer in simplest form.

1.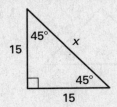

2.

3.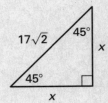

4.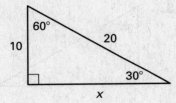

5.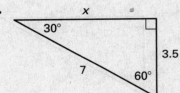

6.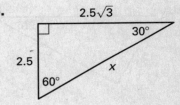

7. How is the length of the hypotenuse in a 30°-60°-90° triangle related to the length of the shorter leg?

LESSON

9.6

Continued

Practice

For use with pages 482–487

Find the unknown lengths. Write your answers in simplest form.

8.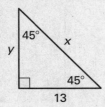

45°
x
y
45°
13

9.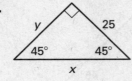

y
25
45°   45°
x

10.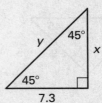

45°
y
x
45°
7.3

11.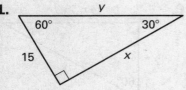

y
60°   30°
15
x

12.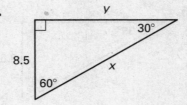

y
30°
8.5
x
60°

13.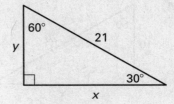

60°
21
y
30°
x

14. A 10-foot tipping trailer is being used to haul gravel. To unload the gravel, the front end of the trailer is raised. How high is the front end of a 10 foot tipping trailer when it is tipped by a 30° angle? by a 45° angle? Round your answers to the nearest foot.

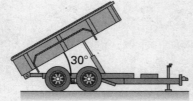

30°

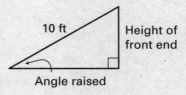

10 ft
Height of
front end
Angle raised

LESSON
9.7

Practice

For use with pages 488–493

Find the tangent of each acute angle. Write your answers as fractions in simplest form.

1.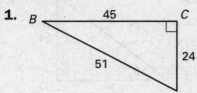

2.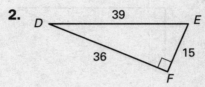

3.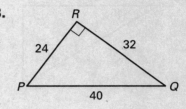

Use a calculator to approximate the tangent value to four decimal places.

4. tan 32°

5. tan 68°

6. tan 43°

7. tan 76°

8. tan 14°

9. tan 82°

Use the table of trigonometric ratios on page 823 to write the value of the tangent.

10. tan 22°

11. tan 56°

12. tan 39°

Name _____   Date _____

Practice

For use with pages 488–493

In Exercises 13–15, find the value of *x*. Round to the nearest tenth.

13.

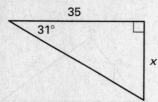

14.

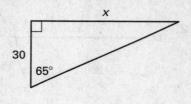

15.

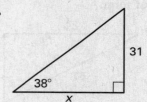

16. A hot air balloon climbs, at a 30° angle to the ground, to a height of
800 feet. To the nearest tenth of a foot, what ground distance has the
balloon traveled to reach 800 feet?

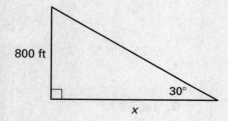

17. You are standing 80 feet from the base of a building.
You estimate that the angle of elevation from your
feet to the top of the building is about 70°. About
how tall is the building?

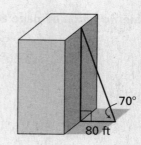

Name _____ Date _____

Practice

For use with pages 494–499

Find the sine and cosine of each acute angle. Write your answers in simplest form.

1.
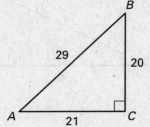

2.
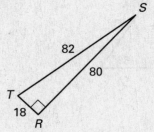

3.
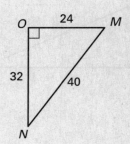

Approximate the sine or cosine value to four decimal places.

4. sin 45°

5. cos 17°

6. sin 25°

7. cos 37°

8. sin 35°

9. cos 58°

10. sin 8°

11. cos 62°

12. sin 44°

Name _____ Date _____

Practice

For use with pages 494–499

Find the value of *x* to the nearest tenth.

13.

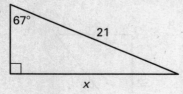

67°

21

x

14.

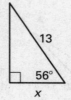

13

56°

x

15.

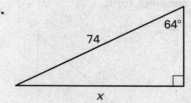

64°

74

x

16.

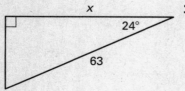

x

24°

63

17.

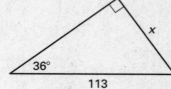

x

36°

113

18.

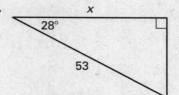

x

28°

53

19. A water slide is 70.3 meters long and makes an angle of 19° with the ground.
To the nearest tenth of a meter, what is the height *h* of the water slide?

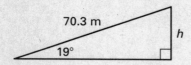

70.3 m

h

19°

Name _____   Date _____

Find the value of x. Then classify the triangle by its angle measures.

1.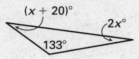
$(x + 20)°$
$2x°$
$133°$

2.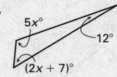
$5x°$
$12°$
$(2x + 7)°$

3.
$(6x - 12)°$
$72°$ $9x°$

4.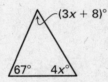
$(3x + 8)°$
$67°$ $4x°$

5.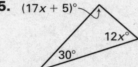
$(17x + 5)°$
$12x°$
$30°$

6.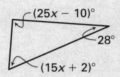
$(25x - 10)°$
$28°$
$(15x + 2)°$

7. The perimeter of an equilateral triangle is 156 feet. Find the length of each side.

8. The perimeter of an isosceles triangle is 89 centimeters. The length of one side is 35 centimeters. The lengths of the other two sides are equal. Find the lengths of the other two sides.

9. The ratio of the angle measures in a triangle is 11 : 14 : 20. Find the angle measures. Then classify the triangle by its angle measures.

Name _____ Date _____

Practice

For use with pages 511–515

Find the unknown side lengths of the triangle given the perimeter P. Then classify the triangle by its side lengths.

10. $P = 51$ in.

11. $P = 64$ yd

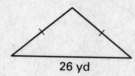

26 yd

12. $P = 93$ cm

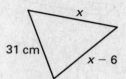

x

31 cm

x − 6

13. The ratio of the side lengths of a triangle is $4 : 7 : 9$. The perimeter of the triangle is 120 feet. Find the side lengths. Then classify the triangle by its side lengths.

14. A sailboat flies the flag of a sailing club. The ratio of the side lengths of the flag is $9 : 9 : 11$. The perimeter of the flag is 116 inches. Find the side lengths. Then classify the triangle by its side lengths.

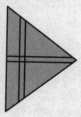

LESSON
10.2

Name _____ Date _____

Practice
For use with pages 516–520

Tell whether the figure is a polygon. If it is a polygon, classify it and tell whether it is *convex* or *concave*. If it is not, explain why.

1.

2.

3.

Classify the quadrilateral.

4.

5.

6.

Find the value of x.

7.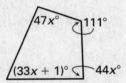
$47x°$ $111°$
$(33x + 1)°$ $44x°$

8.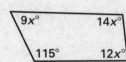
$9x°$ $14x°$
$115°$ $12x°$

9.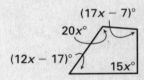
$(17x - 7)°$
$20x°$
$(12x - 17)°$
$15x°$

10.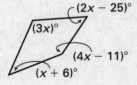
$(2x - 25)°$
$(3x)°$
$(4x - 11)°$
$(x + 6)°$

11.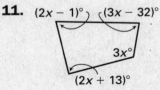
$(2x - 1)°$ $(3x - 32)°$
$3x°$
$(2x + 13)°$

12.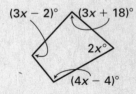
$(3x - 2)°$ $(3x + 18)°$
$2x°$
$(4x - 4)°$

Name _____ Date _____

Practice

For use with pages 516–520

13. A quadrilateral has both pairs of opposite sides parallel. Sketch and classify the quadrilateral.

14. For the trapezoid shown, the ratio $m\angle B : m\angle D$ is $5 : 1$. Write and solve an equation to find the value of x.

LESSON
10.3

Practice

For use with pages 521–526

Find the area of the parallelogram.

1.
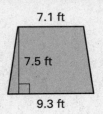
6.2 yd

5.4 yd

2.
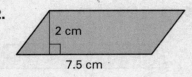
2 cm

7.5 cm

3.
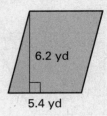
10.8 m

3 m

Find the area of the trapezoid.

4.
7.1 ft
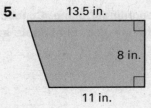
7.5 ft

9.3 ft

5.
13.5 in.

8 in.

11 in.

6.
7 mm
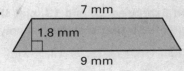
1.8 mm

9 mm

7. The base of a parallelogram is 28.4 centimeters. The height is one fourth of the base. Find the area of the parallelogram.

8. The height of a trapezoid is 13 yards. One of the bases is 2.5 times the height, and the other base is two times the height. Find the area of the trapezoid.

Name _____ Date _____

Practice

For use with pages 521–526

Find the unknown measure of the parallelogram or trapezoid.

9. $A = 36.18 \text{ mm}^2$

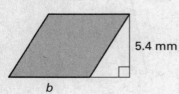

b

5.4 mm

10. $A = 135 \text{ m}^2$

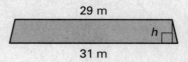

29 m

h

31 m

11. $A = 294 \text{ ft}^2$

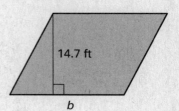

14.7 ft

b

In Exercises 12 and 13, plot the points in a coordinate plane. Connect the points so that they form a polygon. Identify the polygon and find its area.

12. $(-3, 1), (3, 2), (3, -2), (-3, -3)$

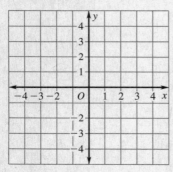

13. $(-5, 4), (-3, 2), (-3, -4), (-5, -4)$

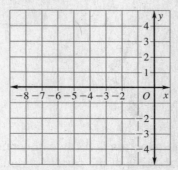

Find the area of the figure.

14.

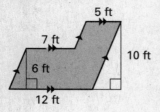

5 ft

7 ft

6 ft

10 ft

12 ft

15.

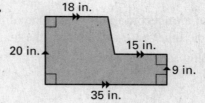

18 in.

20 in.

15 in.

9 in.

35 in.

LESSON

10.4 **Practice**

For use with pages 527–533

Find the circumference of the circle. Use 3.14 or $\frac{22}{7}$ for π. Round to the nearest whole number.

1.

30 m

2.

81 cm

3.

56 in.

4.

26 mm

5.

39 ft

6.

49 yd

For a circle with the given circumference C, find the radius and diameter of the circle. Round to the nearest whole number.

7. $C = 63$ m

8. $C = 91$ ft

9. $C = 132$ in.

Find the area of the circle. Use 3.14 or $\frac{22}{7}$ for π. Round to the nearest whole number.

10.

48 in.

11.

25 cm

12.

38 mm

13.

27 yd

14.

63 m

15.

84 ft

10.4 Practice
Continued

For use with pages 527–533

For a circle with the given area A, find the radius and diameter of the circle. Round to the nearest whole number.

16. $A = 113$ cm^2 **17.** $A = 3018$ ft^2 **18.** $A = 7850$ m^2

19. A manhole cover has a diameter of 24 inches. Find the circumference of the manhole cover to the nearest inch.

20. The base of a yogurt container has a circumference of about 22 centimeters. Find the radius and diameter of the base to the nearest centimeter.

21. Find the shaded area of the basketball court to the nearest foot.

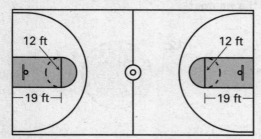

Name _____   Date _____

Practice

For use with pages 537–543

Draw a net for the solid. Then find the surface area. Round to the nearest whole number.

1.

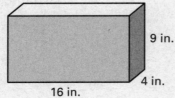

9 in.
16 in.
4 in.

2.

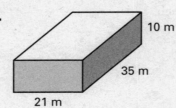

10 m
35 m
21 m

3.

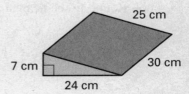

25 cm
30 cm
7 cm
24 cm

4.

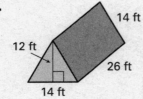

14 ft
12 ft
26 ft
14 ft

5.

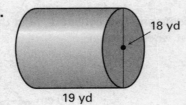

18 yd
19 yd

6.

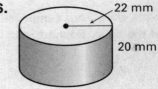

22 mm
20 mm

LESSON
10.5
Continued

Practice
For use with pages 537–543

7. A flower pot is approximately in the shape of a cylinder. The diameter is
10 inches, and the height is 6 inches. Find the surface area of the flower
pot. Round to the nearest square inch.

8. Find the surface area of the bookends shown.

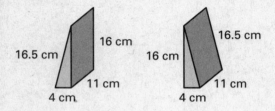

**The solids shown are composed of prisms and half cylinders. Find the surface
area of the solid. Round to the nearest whole number.**

9.

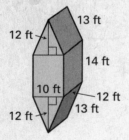

10.

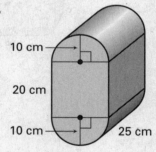

Name _____ Date _____

Practice

For use with pages 544–549

Find the slant height of the pyramid or cone. Round to the nearest tenth.

1.
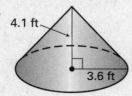
4.1 ft
3.6 ft

2.
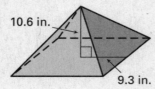
10.6 in.
9.3 in.

3.
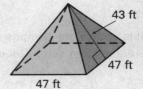
8.6 m
5.7 m

Find the surface area of the regular pyramid.

4.
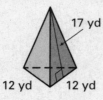
17 yd
12 yd   12 yd
$B \approx 62.4 \text{ yd}^2$

5.
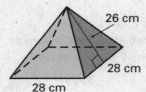
26 cm
28 cm
28 cm

6.
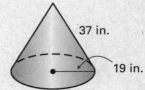
43 ft
47 ft
47 ft

Find the surface area of the cone. Round to the nearest whole number.

7.
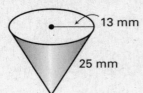
13 mm
25 mm

8.
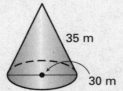
35 m
30 m

9.
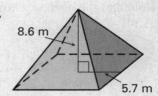
37 in.
19 in.

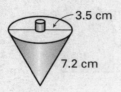

Name _____ Date _____

Practice

For use with pages 544–549

10. The base of a top is shaped like a cone. Find the surface area of the cone. Round to the nearest whole number.

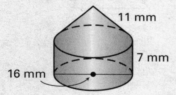

3.5 cm

7.2 cm

The solids shown are composed of cones, cylinders, and pyramids. Find the surface area of the solid. Round to the nearest whole number.

11.

11 mm

7 mm

16 mm

12.

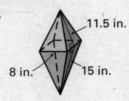

11.5 in.

8 in.

15 in.

Name _____   Date _____

Practice

For use with pages 550–557

Find the volume of the prism or cylinder. Round to the nearest whole number.

1.
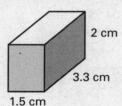
2 cm
3.3 cm
1.5 cm

2.
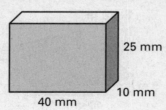
25 mm
10 mm
40 mm

3.
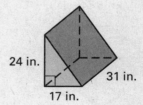
24 in.
31 in.
17 in.

4.
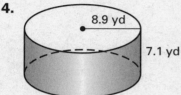
8.9 yd
7.1 yd

5.
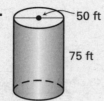
50 ft
75 ft

6.
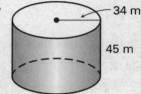
34 m
45 m

7. Find the volume to the nearest millimeter of a cylinder that is 45 millimeters tall and has a diameter of 26 millimeters.

8. You are mailing a gift box that is 18 inches by 8 inches by 12 inches. You want to put it in a larger box and surround it with foam packing. The larger box is 20 inches by 12 inches by 15 inches. How many cubic inches are there for the foam packing?

Name _____ Date _____

Practice

For use with pages 550–557

Find the unknown dimension. Round to the nearest whole number.

9. $V = 57{,}750 \text{ yd}^3$

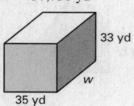

33 yd

w

35 yd

10. $V = 8640 \text{ m}^3$

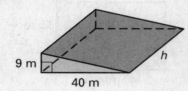

9 m

h

40 m

11. $V = 64{,}795 \text{ mm}^3$

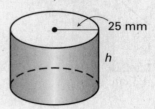

25 mm

h

12. Tell which safe holds more.

Safe A

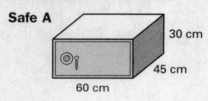

30 cm

45 cm

60 cm

Safe B

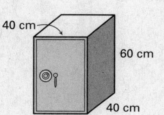

40 cm

60 cm

40 cm

The solids shown are composed of prisms and half cylinders. Find the volume of the solid. Round to the nearest whole number.

13.

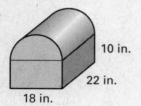

10 in.

22 in.

18 in.

14.

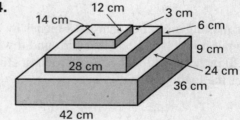

12 cm

14 cm

3 cm

6 cm

9 cm

28 cm

24 cm

36 cm

42 cm

LESSON
10.8 **Practice**
For use with pages 558–563

Find the volume of the pyramid or cone. Round to the nearest whole number.

1.
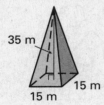
35 m
15 m
15 m

2.
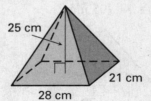
25 cm
21 cm
28 cm

3.
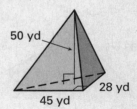
50 yd
28 yd
45 yd

4.
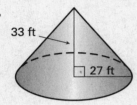
33 ft
27 ft

5.
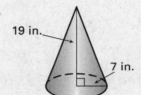
19 in.
7 in.

6.
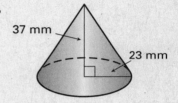
37 mm
23 mm

7. The candles shown are shaped like pyramids. Find the volume to the nearest cubic centimeter of each pyramid. Then tell which candle has the greater volume.

Candle A

Candle B

22 cm
5 cm
5 cm

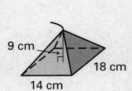
9 cm
18 cm
14 cm

Name _____   Date _____

Practice

For use with pages 558–563

Find the unknown dimension. Round to the nearest whole number.

8. $V = 29{,}744$ yd^3

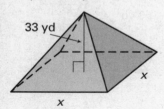

33 yd

x

x

9. $V = 31{,}705$ mm^3

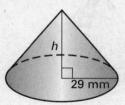

h

29 mm

10. $V = 171{,}597$ m^3

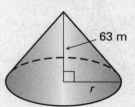

63 m

r

The solid in Exercise 11 is a cylinder with a cone-shaped hole in it. The solid in Exercise 12 is composed of a prism and a pyramid. Find the volume of the solid. Round your answer to the nearest whole number.

11.

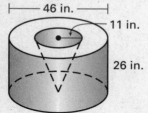

46 in.

11 in.

26 in.

12.

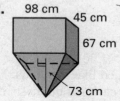

98 cm

45 cm

67 cm

73 cm

LESSON

Name _____ Date _____

11.1 Practice

For use with pages 581–587

Make an ordered stem-and-leaf plot of the data.

1. 16.9, 17.8, 16.3, 16.4, 17.8, 18.1, 15.4, 16.8, 17.1, 18.3, 15.5, 16.2, 17.9

2. 96.9, 92.5, 94.7, 98.4, 92.1, 94.8, 96.4, 97.5, 97.2, 96.8, 97.7, 97.6, 93.0, 94.6, 97.2, 97.8, 94.3, 97.7

3. 282, 274, 250, 291, 286, 249, 289, 288, 251, 261, 272, 268, 247, 263, 248, 267, 295, 287

4. 737, 784, 753, 762, 771, 756, 754, 739, 757, 762, 775, 758, 759, 786, 755, 778, 756, 778, 758

In Exercises 5–8, use the data to make a frequency table and a histogram.

5. 20, 4, 6, 9, 14, 15, 20, 23, 21, 7, 4, 12, 10, 5

6. 24, 42, 44, 39, 21, 30, 31, 35, 33, 30, 34, 36, 34, 37, 33, 38, 22

7. 5300, 3800, 1000, 1900, 2100, 2600, 3100, 5400, 1800, 1600, 2300, 2400, 1700, 2900, 2400, 2200, 5700, 1200, 2300, 2100

8. 281, 241, 267, 290, 283, 281, 282, 284, 262, 271, 274, 285, 261, 284, 283, 280, 275

LESSON
11.1
Continued

Practice

For use with pages 581–587

9. The ages of 30 people who participate in a contest are as follows:
23, 25, 37, 44, 48, 39, 33, 27, 28, 41, 19, 18, 22, 29, 35, 46, 47, 31, 30, 20,
34, 37, 41, 45, 25, 28, 34, 45, 40, 18.

   a. Make an ordered stem-and-leaf plot of the data.

   b. Find the median and range of the data.

Make a histogram from the stem-and-leaf plot. Do not use the same intervals in your histogram as are used in the stem-and-leaf plot.

10.

19	1 2 3 4
20	1 2 5 6 7 8 9
21	0 3 4 6 7 7
22	0 0 3 9 9

Key: $22 \mid 3 = 22.3$

11.

58	1 2 3 3 4 5
59	0 2 4 5 5 6 7 7 8 8 8
60	7 9
61	1 1 3 5 9

Key: $58 \mid 1 = 581$

12. The results of the top ten distances (in meters) for men and women in a long jump competition are listed below.

   Women: 5.20, 5.08, 4.64, 5.76, 5.62, 5.06, 4.75, 4.98, 4.70, 4.76

   Men: 6.39, 6.56, 6.80, 6.97, 6.70, 6.68, 6.50, 6.57, 6.67, 6.59

   a. Make frequency tables for both the men's and women's distances.

   b. Use the frequency tables you made in part (a) to make histograms for the two sets of data.

   c. What conclusions can you make from the distributions of the data?

LESSON
11.2 Practice

For use with pages 588–593

Complete the statement.

1. The interquartile range of a data set is the _____ of the _____ quartile and the _____ quartile.

2. In a box-and-whisker plot, the entire box represents about _____% of the data.

3. In a box-and-whisker plot, one whisker represents about _____% of the data.

Make a box-and-whisker plot of the data.

4. School days missed: 0, 4, 7, 2, 5, 9, 11, 3

5. Fuel economy of small sedans (in miles per gallon):
   51, 41, 38, 42, 35, 32, 29, 30

6. Shoe prices (in dollars): 10, 20, 18, 8, 13, 15, 11, 16, 14, 20, 25, 17, 30

7. Battery life in laptop computers (in hours): 5, 3.75, 4.75, 2.75, 3, 5.5, 4, 3.5

Name _____ Date _____

Practice
For use with pages 588–593

The box-and-whisker plots show the weights of electric handheld power blowers and gasoline handheld power blowers.

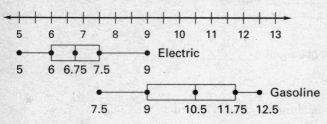

8. Compare the median, range, and interquartile range for the two types of blowers.

9. About what percent of the electric blowers are less than 7.5 pounds? About what percent of the gasoline blowers are more than 10.5 pounds?

10. Which type of blower would you say is the "lighter" blower? Explain.

In Exercises 11–13, use the following information. An outlier is a data value whose distance from the upper or lower quartile is more than 1.5 times the interquartile range.

11. Make a box-and-whisker plot for the following data (snowfall, in inches, of the top ten snowiest cities in the U.S. in a recent year): 100, 129, 105, 97, 112, 103, 241, 110, 117, 98.

12. Determine if there are any outliers in the snowfall data set. Make a box-and-whisker plot for the data, excluding any outliers.

13. What conclusion(s) can you make from the plot in Exercise 12 that you would not make from the plot in Exercise 11?

LESSON
11.3 Practice

For use with pages 596–600

Tell whether the data are *numerical* or *categorical*. Then tell which display(s) you would use to display the data. Explain your reasoning.

1. A survey was conducted where the responses were agree, disagree, and unsure.

2. A zookeeper recorded the weights of the baby animals in the zoo.

3. A study determined the average winning score of high school soccer teams.

4. A meteorologist recorded the amount of rainfall in 3 states over one year.

Tell which data display(s) allow you to identify the specified information.

5. The range of the data set

6. The least value of the data set

7. A teacher records the scores on a project and wants to group the data in intervals of 5 points. Should the teacher use a stem-and-leaf plot or a histogram? Explain.

8. Thirty people were asked to state the number of hours per week that they commute to and from work in a car. The frequency table shows the results.

   a. Is the frequency table misleading? Explain.

   b. What conclusions can you make from the frequency table?

Hours spent commuting		
Interval	Tally	Frequency
0–2 hours	IIII	4
3–5 hours	JHr I	6
6–10 hours	JHr JHr JHr	15
11–12 hours	III	3
13–20 hours	II	2

Name _____   Date _____

Practice
For use with pages 596–600

9. The table shows the number of people (in thousands) attending a tennis tournament in 10 different years.

Tennis Tournament Attendance			
Year	Attendance	Year	Attendance
1980	12.3	1990	17.3
1981	14.1	1992	20.1
1982	20.2	1995	15.9
1985	19.6	1999	21.0
1988	18.4	2000	18.5

a. Make a line graph using every 5th year, starting with 1980. What trend does the graph show?

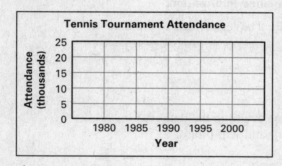

b. Make a new line graph using all the years shown in the table. What trend does it show?

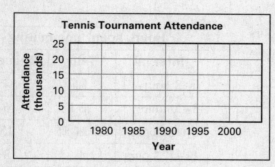

c. Which line graph represents the data more accurately, the one in part (a) or the one in part (b)? Explain.

LESSON 11.4 Practice

For use with pages 601–607

A newspaper is conducting a survey to predict who will win the next mayoral election. Tell whether the sampling method is *random*, *systematic*, *stratified*, *convenience*, or *self-selected*.

1. Set up a phone number where people can call in their opinion.

2. Call every 100th person in the phone book.

3. Interview every fifth person that leaves a grocery store.

4. Interview 10 people from each neighborhood.

In Exercises 5 and 6, describe the population and tell what type of sampling method is used. Then tell whether the sample is likely to represent the population. Explain your answer.

5. A researcher wants to know the opinions that people in a state have about home computers. The researcher asks every third customer who enters a computer store in a mall whether they approve or disapprove of computers at home.

6. A writer for a newspaper wants to determine the most popular non-fiction book among residents in a town. The writer asks every other person leaving the local library what their favorite non-fiction book is.

7. A speaker at a seminar wants to know how well a speech was received by members of the audience. The speaker leaves the form shown on a table for members of the audience to complete after the speech.

  a. Describe the population and the sampling method.

1. Was the information communicated effectively?
2. What did you enjoy most about the speaker?
3. What did you enjoy least about the speaker?

  b. Is the questionnaire likely to represent the population? Explain why or why not.

LESSON 11.4 Practice
Continued

For use with pages 601–607

In Exercises 8–10, tell whether the question is potentially biased. Explain your answer. If the question is biased, rewrite it so that it is not.

8. Do you support building an expensive new stadium while the old one is perfectly usable?

9. How many times a week do you exercise?

10. Don't you think our town should have a fun new park?

11. Researchers conducted a study to determine the average age of the people living in a city. They did so by recording the age of 200 people in the city. Tell whether the following statements, if true, would lower your confidence in the results of the study. Explain your answers.

   a. The researchers chose the people in their sample randomly.

   b. The researchers selected people only from the eastern portion of the city.

   c. Some of the people in the study were much older than others.

LESSON 11.5 Practice

For use with pages 608–613

1. A survey of 300 randomly selected new parents finds that 99 new parents prefer brand A baby food. Predict how many new parents in a town of 2500 new parents prefer brand A baby food.

2. You interview a random sample of 100 residents in a town. Forty-two people say that raspberry is their favorite muffin flavor. There are 3000 people in the town. Predict how many people in the town would say that raspberry is their favorite muffin flavor.

3. Four surveys based on random samples of students in a school were conducted before a school student council election. The results are shown in the table along with the margin of error for each survey. For each election, predict a winner or tell whether the election is too close to call.

Position	Leading Candidate	Trailing Candidate	Margin of Error
President	52%	48%	±4%
Vice President	55%	45%	±4%
Secretary	51%	49%	±5%
Treasurer	53.5%	46.5%	±3%

LESSON
11.5
Continued

Practice
For use with pages 608–613

4. A politician needs 750 signatures from people in town to run for office. You interview a random sample of 100 people in town. You find that 38 people say they would provide their signature. The town has 3200 people. Do you think enough people will provide their signatures? Justify your reasoning.

5. Review the newspaper article below which summarizes the results of a survey. How much trust do you have in the survey? Do you think the conclusions in the article are valid? Explain.

Tamarind, Che, and Loquat Becoming Common Fruits!

A recent survey of 150 people at the local market found more people in town eat tamarind, che, and loquat than eat traditional fruits, such as apples. The survey was conducted by Frank's Fruit Stand, a fruit seller who specializes in unusual fruit.

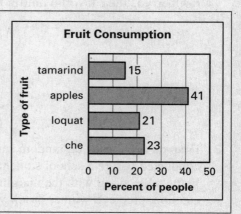

6. A town has 2500 residents. A survey finds that 92 residents out of a random sample of 575 residents have a red car. The margin of error for the survey is ±4%. Find the interval in which the total number of residents with a red car is most likely to lie.

LESSON 11.6 Practice

For use with pages 615–619

1. List all the permutations of the numbers 1, 2, and 3.

2. $6! =$ ____ $\cdot$ ____ $\cdot$ ____ $\cdot$ ____ $\cdot$ ____ $\cdot$ ____

Match the expression with its value

3. $4!$

4. $_4P_1$

5. $0!$

6. $_4P_2$

A. 1

B. 12

C. 4

D. 24

Evaluate the factorial.

7. $(4-1)!$

8. $(10-4)!$

9. $(17-12)!$

10. $(12-4)!$

Find the number of permutations.

11. $_5P_0$

12. $_6P_2$

13. $_{20}P_1$

14. $_7P_3$

15. $_7P_7$

16. $_8P_4$

17. $_{21}P_3$

18. $_{14}P_6$

Name _____ Date _____

Practice
For use with pages 615–619

Write the expression using factorials.

19. $21 \cdot 20 \cdot 19$

20. 45

21. $11 \cdot 10 \cdot 9 \cdot 8 \cdot 7 \cdot 6 \cdot 5 \cdot 4$

22. $53 \cdot 52 \cdot 51 \cdot 50$

23. Ten cyclists enter a race. In how many ways can they finish first, second, and third?

24. A company's security system uses a code consisting of 5 different digits. Your security code has the digits 8, 2, 9, 0, and 3, but you don't remember the order in which the 5 digits are to be entered. Find the probability that you enter the correct code on the first try.

25. In how many ways can 5 children line up in one row to have their picture taken?

26. You have 12 CDs and choose 4 of them to play one evening. How many orders of CDs are possible for playing the 4 CDs?

LESSON

11.7 Practice

For use with pages 620–625

Name _____ Date _____

1. To find the number of combinations of n objects taken r at a time, divide the number of _____ of n objects taken r at a time by _____.

Find the number of combinations.

2. $_4C_1$

3. $_3C_3$

4. $_5C_3$

5. $_7C_2$

6. $_9C_8$

7. $_{14}C_0$

8. $_{12}C_4$

9. $_{13}C_{12}$

10. $_8C_6$

11. $_9C_3$

12. $_{15}C_2$

13. $_{14}C_{10}$

In Exercises 14–16, tell whether the possibilities can be counted using *permutations* **or** *combinations*. **Then answer the question.**

14. A media research firm conducts a survey of television viewers and asks them to state their favorite show and least favorite show from a list of 15 shows. How many possible responses are there?

15. The manager of an engineering department wants to form a three-person advisory committee from the 18 employees in the department. How many different groups can the manager form?

Name _____ Date _____

Practice

For use with pages 620–625

16. There are 4 processes involved in assembling a certain product. These processes can be performed in any order. Management wants to find which order is the least time consuming. How many orders will have to be tested?

17. A company wants to send 3 of its 10 sales representatives to a conference. How many different groups can the company choose?

18. A state government is planning a new section of highway and has received bids from 16 construction companies. The state needs 5 of the companies. How many different groups of 5 companies can the state choose?

19. A jury consists of 8 men and 4 women. Four jurors are selected at random for an interview. How many different groups of 4 jurors are there? Find the probability that all 4 jurors chosen are women.

LESSON

11.8 Practice

For use with pages 626–632

Complete the statement.

1. If A and B are disjoint events, then $P(A \text{ or } B) = $ _____.

2. If A and B are overlapping events, then $P(A \text{ or } B) = $ _____.

3. The sum of the probabilities of complementary events is always _____.

4. If you know the probability of an event A, then the probability of the complementary event, *not* A, is given by $P(\text{not } A) = $ _____.

The spinner is divided into equal parts. For the specified events A and B, tell whether the events are *disjoint* or *overlapping*. Then find *P*(A or B).

5. **Event A:** Stops on an even number.
   Event B: Stops on a shaded sector.

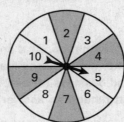

6. **Event A:** Stops on a shaded sector.
   Event B: Stops on a multiple of 5.

Events A and B are disjoint. Find *P*(A or B).

7. $P(A) = \frac{3}{14}, P(B) = \frac{9}{14}$

8. $P(A) = \frac{11}{42}, P(B) = \frac{13}{42}$

Name _____ Date _____

Practice

For use with pages 626–632

Events A and B are overlapping. Find P(A or B).

9. $P(A) = \dfrac{7}{20}$, $P(B) = \dfrac{9}{20}$, $P(A \text{ and } B) = \dfrac{3}{20}$

10. $P(A) = \dfrac{1}{4}$, $P(B) = \dfrac{1}{3}$, $P(A \text{ and } B) = \dfrac{5}{24}$

Given P(A), find P(not A).

11. $P(A) = 27\%$ **12.** $P(A) = 89\%$ **13.** $P(A) = \dfrac{9}{26}$ **14.** $P(A) = \dfrac{13}{41}$

In Exercises 15–17, use the following information. At a college, 51% of the students are women, 25% of the students are business majors, 5% have not chosen a major, and 12% are women and business majors. A student newspaper conducts a poll and selects students at random to answer a survey.

15. What is the probability that a randomly selected student will be either a woman or a business major?

16. What is the probability that a randomly selected student is not a business major?

17. What is the probability that a randomly selected student is either a business major or has not chosen a major?

LESSON
11.9 Practice
For use with pages 633–639

Complete the statement.

1. If A and B are independent events, then $P(A \text{ and } B) =$ _____.

2. If A and B are dependent events, then $P(A \text{ and } B) =$ _____.

Events A and B are independent. Find the missing probability.

3. $P(A) = \frac{2}{5}$

   $P(B) = \frac{1}{6}$

   $P(A \text{ and } B) =$ ____

4. $P(A) = \frac{3}{8}$

   $P(B) = \frac{4}{9}$

   $P(A \text{ and } B) =$ ____

Events A and B are dependent. Find the missing probability.

5. $P(A) = \frac{6}{11}$

   $P(B \text{ given } A) = \frac{1}{2}$

   $P(A \text{ and } B) =$ ____

6. $P(A) = \frac{8}{15}$

   $P(B \text{ given } A) = \frac{5}{14}$

   $P(A \text{ and } B) =$ ____

Practice

For use with pages 633–639

In Exercises 7 and 8, tell whether the events are *independent* or *dependent*. Then find P(A and B).

7. You randomly choose a marble from a bag of 8 green marbles and 5 blue marbles. You randomly draw another marble without replacing the first marble.

   Event A: You draw a blue marble.

   Event B: You draw a blue marble.

8. A weather forecaster says that there is a 25% chance of rain today and a 55% chance of rain tomorrow.

   Event A: It rains today.

   Event B: It rains tomorrow.

9. Each week you have a surprise quiz in your social studies and science classes. Find the probability that both quizzes will be given on the same day next week.

10. Twelve light bulbs are tested to see if they last as long as the manufacturer claims they do. Three light bulbs fail the test. Two light bulbs are selected at random without replacement. Find the probability that both light bulbs (a) failed the test and (b) passed the test.

11. A printing company's bookbinding machine has a probability of 0.5% of producing a defective book. If this machine is used to bind 3 books, find the probability that none of the books are defective. Round your answer to the nearest tenth of a percent.

Name _____ Date _____

Practice

For use with pages 651–655

Tell whether the expression is a polynomial. If it is a polynomial, list its terms and classify it.

1. $15b^3$

2. $9b^{-1} + 12y^2$

3. $2t^2 + 5t - 14$

4. $\frac{x}{8} + 13$

5. $\frac{c^2 - 1}{c}$

6. $\frac{m^2}{5} - 2m + 3$

Find the degree of the polynomial.

7. $w + x + y + z$

8. $17abc$

9. $df + gh + dh$

10. $mn + m^2n^2$

11. $-x^2y^3z^2 + 3$

12. $s^3 - s^2t^2 + t^2$

Write the expression as a polynomial in standard form.

13. $10x + 8 - 4 + 5x$

14. $-9b^3 + 6b - 11b^3 - 3b$

15. $-8y^2 + 6y - 4y^2 - 13y$

16. $12 + 9a - 6a^3 + 7a^2 - 15a + 5a^2$

17. $21p^2 - 16p^3 + 3p^4 + 11p^3 - 9p^4$

18. $-4z^2 + z - 3(8z^2 + 6)$

19. $15 + 8x^2 - 9(7x^3 - 3x)$

20. $17c + 6(c^2 - 5c) - 9c^2$

21. $7d^2 + 10(1 - 6d^2) - 4d$

22. $19x - 5(x^2 - 9x) + 6x^2$

Evaluate the polynomial when $x = -4$.

23. $9x^2 - 3x$

24. $6x^2 - 3x + 13$

25. $x^4 - x^2 + 1$

26. $-2x^3 - 6x^2 + x$

27. $-x^2 + 9x - 21$

28. $81 - 5x^2$

Write a polynomial expression for the perimeter of the figure. Give your answer in standard form.

29.

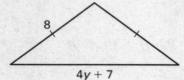

8

$4y + 7$

30.

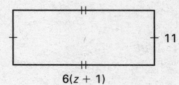

11

$6(z + 1)$

31.

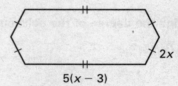

$2x$

$5(x - 3)$

32. For the period 1990–2001, the cost (in dollars) of new privately owned homes in the United States can be approximated by the polynomial $392t^2 + 852t + 120{,}326$, where t is the number of years since 1990.

  a. What is the degree of the polynomial?

  b. Evaluate the polynomial when $t = 0$ to find the approximate cost of new privately owned homes in 1990.

  c. Evaluate the polynomial when $t = 11$ to find the approximate cost of new privately owned homes in 2001.

Evaluate the polynomial when $a = 2$ and $b = -3$.

33. $a^2 - ab^3 + 1$

34. $b^3 + 2ab + a^3$

35. $b^4 - 49$

36. $a^4 - a^2b$

37. $5a^2 + 4b^3$

38. $-2a^2 + a^2b^3$

Name _____ Date _____

Practice
For use with pages 656–661

Find the sum.

1. $(-9x^2 - x + 2) + (4x^2 + 2x - 7)$

2. $(-c^2 + 8c - 15) + (c^2 - 5c - 6)$

3. $(w^3 + 6w) + (-w^2 - 8w + 7)$

4. $(-8a^3 + a - 16) + (a^2 + 9a)$

5. $(-10v^2 + 20) + (v^2 - 12v)$

6. $(4n^2 - 13n) + (-n^2 - 5)$

7. $(1.4b^2 + 0.4b - 2.1) + (3.4b^2 - 1.2b + 3.8)$

Find the perimeter of the triangle, rectangle, or square.

8.

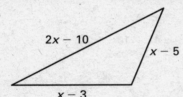
$2x - 10$ $x - 5$ $x - 3$

9.

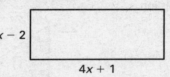
$x - 2$ $4x + 1$

10.

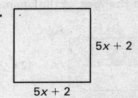
$5x + 2$ $5x + 2$

11. A factory makes two different types of cereal bars. The number of Type A cereal bars that are output in a day is approximated by the polynomial $-2.272t^2 + 89.24t + 52.1$, and the number of Type B cereal bars that are output in a day is approximated by the polynomial $50.31t - 1.5$, where t is the time in hours. Write a polynomial that gives the combined number of cereal bars that are output in a day.

Name _____ Date _____

Practice

For use with pages 656–661

Find the difference.

12. $(15m^2 + 2m - 9) - (-m^2 - 12m - 6)$ **13.** $(11t^2 - 8t - 19) - (20t^2 + 3t + 10)$

14. $(4b^3 - 7b - 7) - (b^2 + 6b - 12)$ **15.** $(-x^2 - 5x + 9) - (2x^3 + 8x - 13)$

16. $(15h^4 + 14) - (3h^4 - 4)$ **17.** $(3n^4 + 6n + 1) - (9n^4 + 7n^2 - 18)$

18. $(0.7a^2 - 1.8a + 1.4) - (5.6a^2 - 1.2a + 3.7)$

19. $(-2.4z^2 + 9.4z - 0.6) - (9.1z^2 + 6.5z - 4.2)$

Write an expression to represent the area of the shaded region given the total area and the area of the unshaded region.

20.
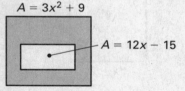
$A = 3x^2 + 9$
$A = 12x - 15$

21.
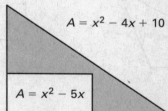
$A = x^2 - 4x + 10$
$A = x^2 - 5x$

22. The number of people in the U.S. employed by the railroad transportation industry during the years 1997–2001 is approximated by the polynomial $-0.83x^3 + 20.4x^2 - 162x + 650$, where x is the year with $x = 7$ corresponding to 1997. The number of people in the U.S. employed by the railroad and water transportation industries combined is approximated by the polynomial $-1.33x^3 + 35.0x^2 - 295x + 1220$. Write a polynomial that gives the number of people in the U.S. employed by the water transportation industry.

LESSON
12.3 **Practice**

For use with pages 662–666

Find the product.

1. $(16y^2 + 4y)11y$

2. $(20h^3 - 18h^2)(-2h)$

3. $(-25z^4 - 7z^2)(-3z)$

4. $12x(x^2 + 3x - 9)$

5. $9c(21c^2 + 24c + 25)$

6. $(15p^2 - 8p - 29)(-6p)$

7. $m(5m^2 + 7m - n)$

8. $(13b + c - 3)6c$

9. $(10y + 15x + 17)xy$

10. $(3ab - 4b - a^2)(-ab)$

11. $-6g(-g^2 + 9h^2 - h)$

12. $(xy - x^2 + 5y)xy$

Find the quotient.

13. $\dfrac{39t^2 + 52t}{13t}$

14. $\dfrac{-42w^3 - 56w^2}{-14w}$

15. $\dfrac{-51x^5 - 34x^4}{17x^3}$

16. $\dfrac{81y^6 - 27y^5 + 9y^4}{-18y^3}$

17. $\dfrac{40b^4 - 32b^3 - 24b}{-8b}$

18. $\dfrac{-105z^7 - 126z^5 + 84z^3}{21z^2}$

19. $\dfrac{-92a^8 - 46a^6 - 115a^3}{23a^3}$

20. $\dfrac{8rt - 4rt + r^3t}{2r}$

21. $\dfrac{20m^2n^2 + 35m^4n - 15mn^3}{5mn}$

Name _____ Date _____

Practice

For use with pages 662–666

22. Write a polynomial expression for the area of the figure. Give your answer in standard form.

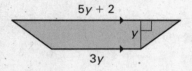

23. You have 16 yards of mesh screen material that you want to use in a rectangular enclosed porch. Let ℓ represent the length of the porch.

   a. Write a polynomial expression for the width in terms of ℓ. Write a polynomial for the area in terms of ℓ.

   b. Draw a diagram of the enclosed porch.

   c. What is the area of the enclosed porch if $\ell = 2$? if $\ell = 3$?

24. The length of a picture frame is 12 inches less than twice the width of the frame. Let w be the width of the picture frame. Write a polynomial expression in terms of w for the area of the picture frame. Give your answer in standard form.

Name _____ Date _____

Practice

For use with pages 667–672

Find the product.

1. $(8n - 3)(n - 7)$

2. $(9x + 5)(3x - 6)$

3. $(-2a - 1)(-4a - 8)$

4. $(-6b + 9)(8b - 1)$

5. $(7y - 10)(2y - 11)$

6. $(12c + 5)(-6c - 2)$

7. $(-z + 2.1)(3z + 3)$

8. $\left(\frac{1}{2}p - 16\right)\left(2p - \frac{1}{4}\right)$

9. $\left(-10h + \frac{5}{4}\right)\left(\frac{2}{3}h - 1\right)$

10. $(6x - y)(4x + 3y)$

11. $(9c - 2d)(3c - 7d)$

12. $(-11a - 8b)(-5a - 6b)$

Complete the table.

13.

	$-2x$	-17
$9x$	$-18x^2$	
-13		221

14.

	____	8
$-15x$	$-45x^2$	$-120x$
10	$30x$	

15.

	$20x$	____
____	$-140x^2$	$-98x$
-18	$-360x$	-252

Name _____ Date _____

Practice

For use with pages 667–672

Write a polynomial expression for the area of the figure. Give your answer in standard form.

16.

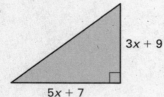

$3x + 9$

$5x + 7$

17.

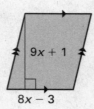

$9x + 1$

$8x - 3$

18.

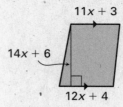

$11x + 3$

$14x + 6$

$12x + 4$

19. The length of a rectangular garden is 5 times the width. A stone walkway 3 feet wide surrounds the garden. Write a polynomial expression for the area of the garden and walkway. Give your answer in standard form.

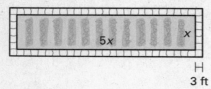

$5x$ x

3 ft

20. The figure shown is composed of a triangle and a rectangle. Write a polynomial expression for the area of the figure. Give your answer in standard form.

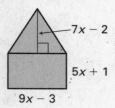

$7x - 2$

$5x + 1$

$9x - 3$

LESSON
12.5 Practice
For use with pages 674–678

Simplify the expression. Write your answer using positive exponents.

1. $(mn)^7$

2. $(7t)^4$

3. $(-6a)^5$

4. $(xy)^9$

5. $\left(\dfrac{w}{10}\right)^6$

6. $\left(\dfrac{-4}{p}\right)^4$

7. $\left(\dfrac{-3}{q}\right)^5$

8. $\left(\dfrac{b}{-9}\right)^3$

9. $(8^2)^{-3}$

10. $(10^5)^4$

11. $(c^7)^{-4}$

12. $(z^6)^8$

LESSON 12.5 Continued

Practice

For use with pages 674–678

Simplify the expression. Write your answer in scientific notation. Round the decimal part of your answer to the nearest hundredth.

13. $(3.5 \times 10^4)^3$

14. $(2.2 \times 10^{-10})^5$

15. $(1.9 \times 10^5)^2$

16. $(2.1 \times 10^{-3})^8$

17. $(5.3 \times 10^4)^9$

18. $(4.6 \times 10^{-6})^7$

19. A test has 2 parts. Part A has 10 true-false questions and part B has 10 multiple choice questions. The questions in part A can be answered in 2^{10} ways and the questions in part B can be answered in 4^{10}, or $(2^2)^{10}$, ways. How many ways are there to answer all 20 questions?

20. Find the volume of a cube that has side length 2.3×10^{-2} meter. Write your answer in scientific notation. Round the decimal part of your answer to the nearest hundredth.

Name _____ Date _____

Practice
For use with pages 679–685

Make a table of values for the given function.

1. $y = 9x^2 + 3x - 10$

2. $y = -7x^2 + 5x - 13$

3. $y = -6x^2 - 2x - 8$

4. $y = x^2 - 4x + 11$

5. $y = -x^2 - 14x - 19$

6. $y = \frac{1}{3}x^2 + 6x - 18$

Match the function with its graph.

7.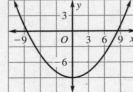

8.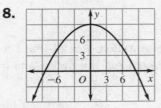

9.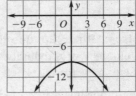

A. $y = -\frac{1}{8}x^2 - 9$

B. $y = \frac{1}{8}x^2 - 9$

C. $y = -\frac{1}{8}x^2 + 9$

Make a table of values for the given function. Then graph the function.

10. $y = -6x^2 - 16$

11. $y = -x^2 + 9x - 11$

12. $y = 4x^2 + 4x + 2$

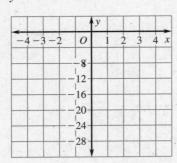

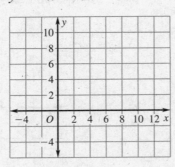

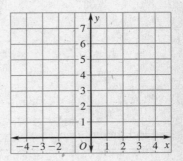

13. $y = \frac{1}{6}x^2 - 2x$

14. $y = -\frac{1}{4}x^2 + 8x$

15. $y = -\frac{1}{2}x^2 - 7x$

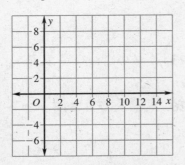

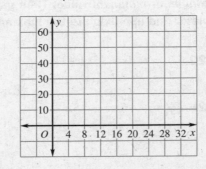

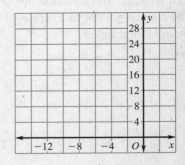

Name _____ Date _____

Practice

For use with pages 679–685

16. $y = \frac{1}{5}x^2 - 15$

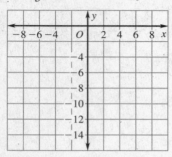

17. $y = -x^2 + x - 1$

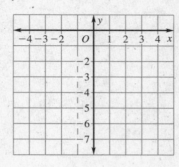

18. $y = -2x^2 + 3x$

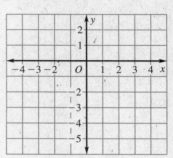

In Exercises 19 and 20, use the following information. Recall that the formula for the volume V of a cylinder is $V = \pi r^2 h$, where r is the radius and h is the height. Use 3.14 for π.

19. A cylinder has a fixed height of 6 units. The radius can vary. Write a formula for the volume of this cylinder as a function of its radius. Make a table of values for zero and whole number values of r. Graph the function.

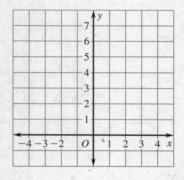

20. A cylinder has a fixed radius of 2 units. The height can vary. Write a formula for the volume of this cylinder as a function of its height. Make a table of values for zero and whole number values of h. Graph the function.

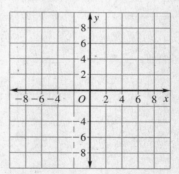

Tell whether the function has a *maximum* or *minimum* value. Then graph the function using a graphing calculator and approximate the maximum or minimum value.

21. $y = -x^2 + 9x + 8$

22. $y = -6x^2 + 7x + 1$

23. $y = 9x^2 - 3x + 2$

24. $y = 7x^2 - 4x + 1$

25. $y = -16x^2 + 75x$

26. $y = -3x^2 + 21x - 24$

Name _____ Date _____

Practice

For use with pages 686–691

Make a table of values for the given function.

1. $y = 3(6)^x$

2. $y = 7(5)^x$

3. $y = 8\left(\dfrac{1}{6}\right)^x$

4. $y = 4\left(\dfrac{1}{12}\right)^x$

5. $y = \dfrac{1}{4}(7)^x$

6. $y = \dfrac{1}{7}(3)^x$

Graph the function.

7. $y = 5^x$

8. $y = 9^x$

9. $y = 4(9)^x$

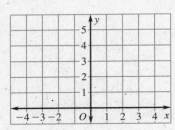

10. $y = 3(4)^x$

11. $y = 8(2)^x$

12. $y = 3\left(\dfrac{1}{9}\right)^x$

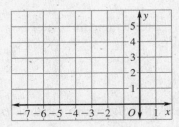

13. $y = 6\left(\dfrac{1}{12}\right)^x$

14. $y = 4\left(\dfrac{1}{2}\right)^x$

15. $y = 5\left(\dfrac{1}{8}\right)^x$

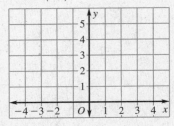
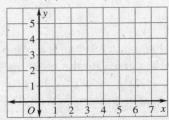
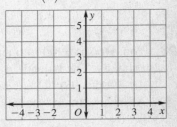

**Use a graphing calculator to graph the function. Then tell whether the function
is an example of** *exponential growth* **or** *exponential decay.*

16. $y = (0.7)^x$

17. $y = 3(0.9)^x$

18. $y = 4(3.1)^x$

Name _____ Date _____

Practice

For use with pages 686–691

Match the function with its graph.

19. $y = \frac{1}{2}(3)^x$

20. $y = 2\left(\frac{1}{3}\right)^x$

21. $y = \frac{1}{3}(2)^x$

A.

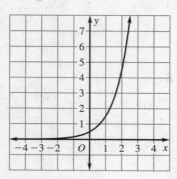

B.

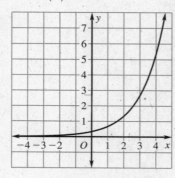

C.

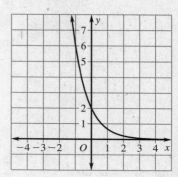

22. A citywide youth basketball tournament has 64 teams at the start. After each round, half the teams are eliminated. The number of teams remaining at the end of each round is given by the function $y = 64\left(\frac{1}{2}\right)^x$ where x is the number of rounds played.

  a. Make a table of values for the function.

  b. After how many rounds do only 2 teams remain? After how many rounds does only 1 team remain?

  c. Suppose the tournament started with 256 teams instead of 64. After how many rounds would only 1 team remain?

23. You deposit $900 into an account that earns 8% interest compounded annually. The balance A after t years is given by the function $A = 900(1.08)^t$. Use a calculator to make a table of values for the function. After how many years will the balance be greater than $1700?

LESSON
12.8 **Practice**
For use with pages 692–697

1. Describe and correct the error in graphing the sequence $-3, 6, -12, 24, \ldots$.

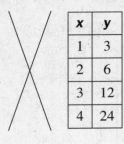

x	y
1	3
2	6
3	12
4	24

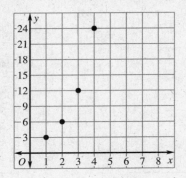

Tell whether the sequence is *arithmetic* or *geometric*. Then find the common difference or the common ratio, and write the next three terms.

2. $-8, -3, 2, 7, \ldots$

3. $-21, -9, 3, 15, \ldots$

4. $48, 42, 36, 30, \ldots$

5. $128, -64, 32, -16, \ldots$

6. $200, 20, 2, 0.2, \ldots$

7. $150, 131, 112, 93, \ldots$

8. $324, 216, 144, 96, \ldots$

9. $\frac{2}{8}, -1, 4, -16, \ldots$

10. $\frac{18}{25}, -3\frac{3}{5}, 18, -90, \ldots$

11. $20, 18.5, 17, 15.5, \ldots$

12. $-13, -25, -37, -49, \ldots$

13. $3125, 1250, 500, 200, \ldots$

Name _____ Date _____

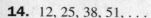

For use with pages 692–697

Tell whether the sequence is *arithmetic* or *geometric*. Write the next three terms of the sequence. Then graph the sequence.

14. 12, 25, 38, 51, . . .

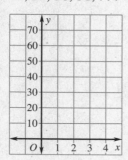

15. 9, 36, 144, 576, . . .

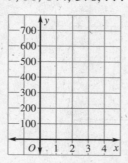

16. 1296, 432, 144, 48, . . .

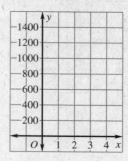

17. 511, 486, 461, 436, . . .

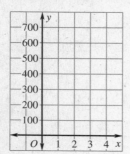

18. 16, 72, 324, 1458, . . .

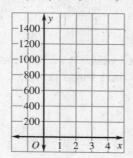

19. 124, 117, 110, 103, . . .

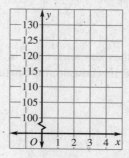

Write the next three terms of the arithmetic sequence. Then write a variable expression for the nth term and evaluate it for $n = 14$.

20. 63, 48, 33, 18, . . .

21. $-4, -1.6, 0.8, 3.2, . . .$

22. 9, 31, 53, 75, . . .

Write the next three terms of the geometric sequence. Then write a variable expression for the nth term and evaluate it for $n = 8$.

23. 900, 90, 9, 0.9, . . .

24. 1, 7, 49, 343, . . .

25. 2187, 729, 243, 81, . . .

26. A bike rental shop charges \$5 for the first hour, and \$2.50 for each additional hour that you rent a bike. Consider the sequence that gives the per hour cost to rent a bike.

a. Write the first 6 terms of the sequence.

b. Write a variable expression for the cost of an h hour bike ride.

c. Markus rented a bike from this shop and paid \$25. For how long did Markus rent the bike?

Name _____ Date _____

Practice
For use with pages 709–713

Tell whether the angles are *complementary*, *supplementary*, or *neither*.

1. $m\angle 1 = 26.5°$
$m\angle 2 = 63.5°$

2. $m\angle 3 = 108.2°$
$m\angle 4 = 61.8°$

3. $m\angle 5 = 32.1°$
$m\angle 6 = 67.9°$

4. $m\angle 7 = 98.7°$
$m\angle 8 = 81.3°$

5. $m\angle 9 = 41.2°$
$m\angle 10 = 58.8°$

6. $m\angle 11 = 27.5°$
$m\angle 12 = 152.5°$

Find $m\angle 1$.

7.
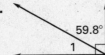

8.

9.
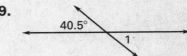

Find the value of x. Then find the unknown angle measure.

10.

11.

12.
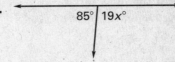

13.
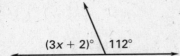

14.
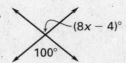

15.
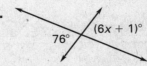

Name _____ Date _____

Practice

For use with pages 709–713

Use the given information to find m∠2.

16. ∠1 and ∠2 are complementary angles, and $m\angle 1 = 19.5°$.

17. ∠1 and ∠2 are supplementary angles, and $m\angle 1 = 87.9°$.

18. ∠1 and ∠2 are vertical angles, and $m\angle 1 = 45.6°$.

In the diagram, write an expression in terms of x for the indicated angle.

19. $m\angle 1$

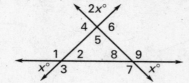

20. $m\angle 4$

21. $m\angle 5$

22. $m\angle 8$

23. On the map, Elm Road intersects both Main Street and South Avenue. ∠1 and ∠3 are complementary angles and $m\angle 2 = 140.5°$. Find $m\angle 1$, $m\angle 3$, and $m\angle 4$.

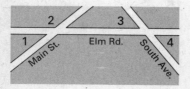

LESSON

13.2 Practice

For use with pages 716–720

In Exercises 1–3, use the diagram at the right.

1. Name all pairs of corresponding angles.

2. Name all pairs of alternate interior angles.

3. Name all pairs of alternate exterior angles.

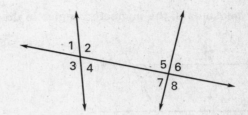

In Exercises 4–6, use the diagram at the right.

4. Name all angles that have the same measure as $\angle 1$.

5. Name all angles that have the same measure as $\angle 2$.

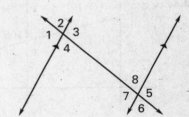

6. If $m\angle 1 = 77°$, find the measures of the other numbered angles in the diagram.

Find the value of x that makes lines m and n parallel.

7.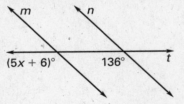

8.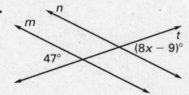

9.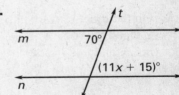

Name _____ Date _____

Practice

For use with pages 716–720

Find the measures of the numbered angles in the diagram.

10.

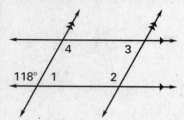

11.

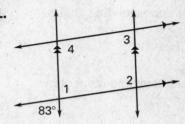

12.

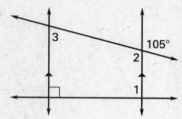

13.

14. A transversal intersects two parallel lines, forming alternate exterior angles
∠1 and ∠2 and corresponding angles ∠1 and ∠3. Illustrate the situation.
How are ∠2 and ∠3 related? How are $m\angle 2$ and $m\angle 3$ related? Explain.

LESSON
13.3 Practice

For use with pages 721–727

In Exercises 1–3, find the measure of an interior angle and the measure of an exterior angle for the regular polygon.

1. 9-gon

2. 12-gon

3. 15-gon

4. For the quadrilateral shown, what is the measure of an exterior angle at vertex *A*? at vertex *B*? at vertex *C*? at vertex *D*?

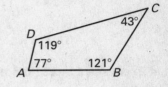

Find the sum of the measures of the interior angles of the polygon.

5.

6.

7.

In Exercises 8 and 9, find the unknown angle measure.

8.

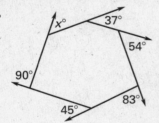

9.

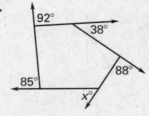

Name _____ Date _____

Practice

For use with pages 721–727

10. The diagram shows the base of the Bellville Turnverein Pavilion. The base of the pavilion is a 12-gon. What is the sum of the measures of the interior angles of the base?

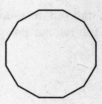

In Exercises 11–13, find the values of x and y.

11.

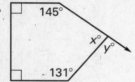

12.

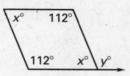

13.

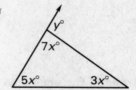

14. The stained glass window is made with polygons. Each shaded figure is a regular polygon. Find the values of x and y.

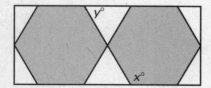

Name _____ Date _____

Describe the translation from the solid figure to the dashed figure in words.

1.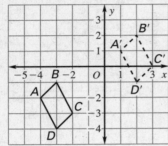

2.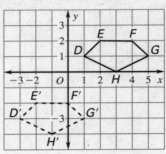

The vertices of a polygon are given. Draw the polygon. Then find the coordinates of the vertices of the image after the specified translation and draw the image.

3. $J(4, 2)$, $K(7, 2)$,
   $L(7, 0)$, $M(5, 0)$;
   $(x, y) \rightarrow (x - 6, y + 5)$

   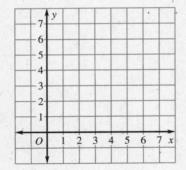

4. $Q(2, -4)$, $R(4, -3)$,
   $S(4, -5)$, $T(2, -7)$,
   $U(1, -6)$;
   $(x, y) \rightarrow (x - 5, y + 2)$

   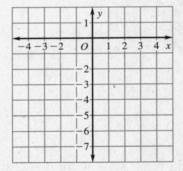

5. $A(-4, 2)$, $B(-2, 5)$,
   $C(0, 3)$, $D(0, 0)$,
   $E(-2, 0)$;
   $(x, y) \rightarrow (x + 4, y)$

   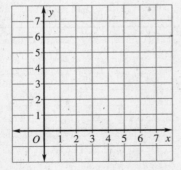

6. $T(-5, 3)$, $V(-4, 2)$,
   $W(-2, 2)$, $X(-1, 3)$,
   $Y(-2, 4)$, $Z(-4, 4)$;
   $(x, y) \rightarrow (x + 4, y - 3)$

   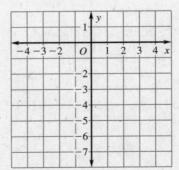

Name _____   Date _____

Practice

For use with pages 729–733

7. The person in the diagram walks down the stairs. Describe the change in the position after the person walks down the stairs.

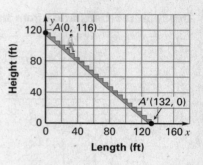

Tell whether you can create a tessellation using only translations of the given polygon. If you can, create a tessellation. If not, explain why not.

8.

9.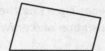

10.

11. Draw $\triangle ABC$ with vertices $A(-4, 4)$, $B(-2, 0)$, and $C(-7, -1)$. Let $\triangle A'B'C'$ be the image of $\triangle ABC$, and let $\triangle A''B''C''$ be the image of $\triangle A'B'C'$.

a. Draw $\triangle A'B'C'$ using the translation $(x, y) \rightarrow (x + 1, y - 6)$.

b. Draw $\triangle A''B''C''$ using the translation $(x, y) \rightarrow (x + 5, y + 3)$.

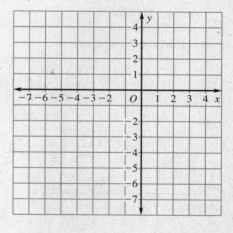

c. How could you move $\triangle ABC$ to $\triangle A''B''C''$ using only one translation?

Name _____ Date _____

Practice

For use with pages 734–739

Find the coordinates of the vertices of the final image after the specified transformations, and draw the final image.

1. Reflect the polygon in the *x*-axis, then translate the image using $(x, y) \rightarrow (x + 5, y + 5)$.

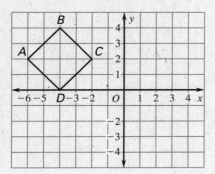

2. Reflect the polygon in the *y*-axis, then translate the image using $(x, y) \rightarrow (x + 4, y - 4)$.

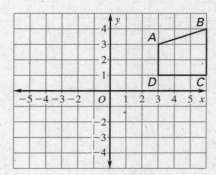

Draw the image of the figure after the specified reflection.

3. Reflect in the line $x = 2$.

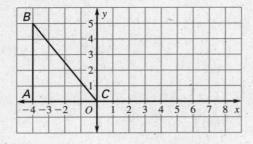

4. Reflect in the line $x = -6$.

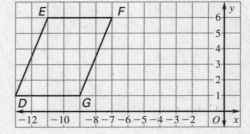

Name _____ Date _____

Practice
For use with pages 734–739

5. Reflect in the line $y = 1$.

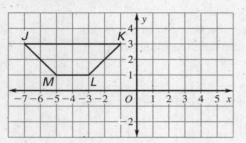

6. Reflect in the line $y = -2$.

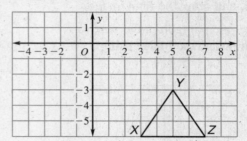

Tell how many lines of symmetry the figure has.

7.

8.

9.

Name _____ Date _____

Practice

For use with pages 740–746

Tell whether the transformation is a rotation about the origin. If so, give the angle and direction of rotation.

1.

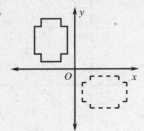

2.

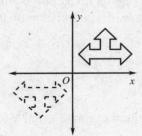

3.

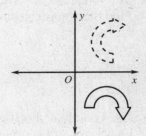

The vertices of a polygon are given. Draw the polygon. Then find the coordinates of the vertices of the image under the specified rotation, and draw the image.

4. $A(-6, 2)$, $B(-5, 4)$,
$C(-2, 3)$, $D(-5, 1)$;
180° rotation

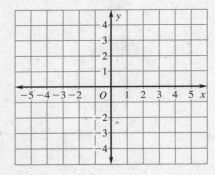

5. $J(0, 0)$, $K(0, 3)$,
$L(4, 4)$, $M(5, 0)$;
90° clockwise rotation

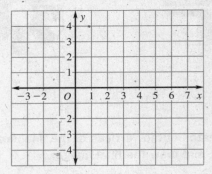

6. $P(1, -2)$, $Q(2, 0)$,
$R(4, -1)$, $S(4, -3)$,
$T(2, -3)$;
180° rotation

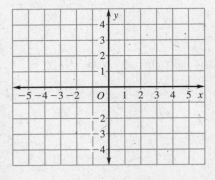

7. $V(-6, -5)$, $W(-4, -2)$,
$X(-1, 0)$, $Y(0, -2)$,
$Z(-3, -3)$;
90° counterclockwise rotation

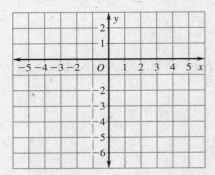

Name _____ Date _____

Practice
For use with pages 740–746

8. Draw △*LMN* with vertices *L*(1, 3), *M*(4, 5), and *N*(3, 1).

    a. You rotate △*LMN* 180°, then you rotate its image 90° counterclockwise. Find the coordinates of the final image. Then draw the image.

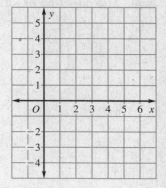

    b. Use coordinate notation to describe how to rotate △*LMN* to the final image in part (a) using one rotation.

Tell whether the figure has rotational symmetry. If so, give each angle and direction of rotation that produce rotational symmetry.

9.

10.

11.

Find the coordinates of the vertices of the final image after the specified transformations, and draw the final image.

12. Rotate the polygon 180°, then reflect the image in the *x*-axis.

13. Rotate the polygon 90° clockwise, then reflect the image in the *y*-axis.

14. Rotate the polygon 90° counterclockwise, then translate the image using $(x, y) \rightarrow (x - 4, y + 3)$.

Name _____ Date _____

The vertices of a polygon are given. Draw the polygon. Then find the coordinates of the vertices of the image after a dilation having the given scale factor, and draw the image.

1. $A(-2, -2)$, $B(-2, 2)$,
$C(3, 4)$, $D(3, -2)$;
$k = 1.5$

2. $W(-4, -6)$, $X(-4, 2)$,
$Y(2, 0)$, $Z(4, -4)$;
$k = \frac{5}{4}$

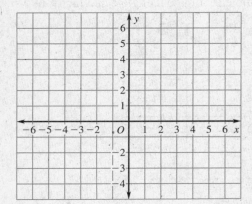

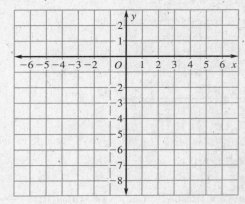

3. $J(2, 8)$, $K(2, -2)$,
$L(6, 0)$, $M(8, 4)$,
$N(6, 8)$;
$k = 0.25$

4. $Q(0, 0)$, $R(0, -2.5)$,
$S(-7.5, -7.5)$, $T(-12.5, -5)$,
$U(-5, 0)$;
$k = \frac{4}{5}$

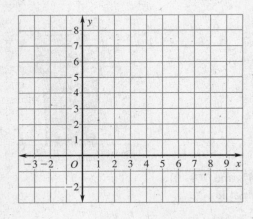

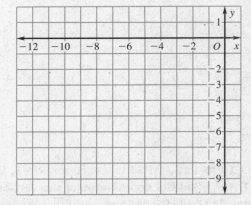

5. Given $\overline{AB}$ with endpoints $A(0, 5)$ and $B(5, 5)$, let $\overline{A'B'}$ with endpoints $A'(0, 5)$ and $B'(3, 5)$ be the image of $\overline{AB}$ after a dilation. What is the scale factor of the dilation?

6. Given $\overline{FG}$ with endpoints $F(3, -2)$ and $G(3, 4)$, let $\overline{F'G'}$ with endpoints $F'(19.5, -13)$ and $G'(19.5, 26)$ be the image of $\overline{FG}$ after a dilation. What is the scale factor of the dilation?

Name _____ Date _____

Practice

For use with pages 747–751

In Exercises 7 and 8, the vertices of a polygon are given. Draw the polygon. Then find the coordinates of the vertices of the final image after the given dilations having the given scale factors, and draw the final image.

7. $\triangle DEF$ has vertices $D(-2, -1)$, $E(0, 2)$, and $F(2, -1)$. You dilate $\triangle DEF$ using a scale factor of 4, and then you dilate its image using a scale factor of 0.5.

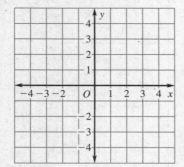

8. Rectangle $ABCD$ has vertices $A(-4, -2)$, $B(-4, 4)$, $C(2, 4)$, and $D(2, -2)$. You dilate $ABCD$ using a scale factor of 1.5, and then you dilate its image using a scale factor of 1.5.

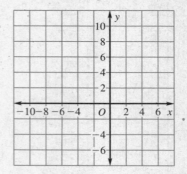

9. A restaurant offers four sizes of soft drinks—small, medium, large and extra-large. The figure shows the medium-sized soft drink. Draw the images of the outline after dilations having the scale factors $\frac{1}{2}$, $1\frac{1}{2}$, and 2, which represent the small, large, and extra-large sizes, respectively.

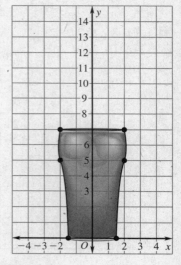

In Exercises 10 and 11, $\triangle RST$ has vertices $R(-3, 0)$, $S(-1, 4)$, and $T(0, 0)$. Draw $\triangle RST$. Then find the coordinates of the vertices of the final image after the specified transformations, and draw the final image.

10. Dilate $\triangle RST$ using a scale factor of 2, then translate its image using $(x, y) \longrightarrow (x + 7, y - 3)$.

11. Dilate $\triangle RST$ using a scale factor of 0.5, then rotate its image 90° clockwise about the origin.

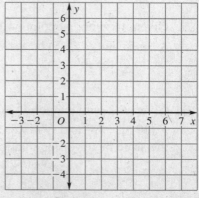